East Anglian Witches and Wizards

East Anglian Witches and Wizards

Michael Howard

WITCHCRAFT OF THE BRITISH ISLES SERIES
BOOK 4

Three Hands Press
2017

First edition published by Three Hands Press June, 2017.

Cover and jacket design by Bob Eames.
Interior book design and typesetting by Joseph Uccello.

ISBN 978-1-945147-04-3 (softcover)
Printed in the United States of America.
threehandspress.com

CONTENTS

1

The Witch Country

THE MODERN NAME of East Anglia, comprising several counties in eastern England, comes from the ancient Anglo-Saxon kingdom of the East Angles. Originally it was the area of Britain that was occupied in the Iron Age by the Iceni tribe. Its most famous leader was the warrior queen Boudicca, who led a failed revolt against the Roman occupation forces. After the Roman legions withdrew from Britain in 410 CE Germanic mercenaries began to arrive in the area. Between 499 and 550 CE the region was occupied by foreign settlers including Jutes from Jutland, Angles from an area south of Denmark and Saxons from Saxony in Germany.

At first East Anglia comprised only the modern counties of Norfolk and Suffolk and in the 6th century it was the tribal land of the North Folk and the South Folk from which their names derive. However with the marriage of Princess Etheldreda, the queen of Northumbria, to King Egfrid, Elig (Anglo-Saxon for 'eel island') the Isle of Ely became part of the region. In 673 Queen Etheldreda founded an abbey and was its abbess until her death six years later when she was made a saint. In the medieval period a cathedral was built at Ely in the middle of the surrounding fens or marshes. Today the county of Cambridgeshire and sometimes Lincolnshire are included in East Anglia.

In the early 7th century East Anglia came under the control of the kingdom of Mercia until a rebellion in 9th century restored its independence. This period of freedom was short lived as in 869 King Edmund was savagely killed by the invading Danish Vikings in what some writers regard as a ritualistic death. He was tied to a tree, scourged,

7

shot with arrows and then beheaded. The body of the king was buried secretly in a wood by his killers, but according to the legend his followers were led to the spot by a talking wolf. After his death Edmund was canonized and became the patron saint of England until he was replaced by the foreign St George. With the peace agreement between King Alfred and the Danes, East Anglia came under 'Danelaw.' In the 11th century Cnut or Canute, the king of both Denmark and England, gave control of the region to Thorkell the Tall, who became the jarl or lord of East Anglia. With the Norman Conquest in 1066 East Anglia had new masters from Normandy in France.

The geography of East Anglia is notable for the flatness of the land and in the winter icy east winds from as far away as Siberia sweep across it from the North Sea. When they are to be found in the county, hills are a rare feature of the landscape. Cambridgeshire is known for its fenlands or marshes and the Norfolk and Suffolk Broads are a series of waterways. They are the result of peat cutting in the Middle Ages and the subsequent drainage of the waterlogged land in the 17th century by Dutch engineers. The land was then used for arable farming, animal grazing and reed cutting for thatching roofs. The main crop grown was wheat and Norfolk soon became known as 'the breadbasket of England'. There used to be 400 windmills in the county, but only one survives today. In modern times the Broads became a popular destination for tourists hiring and sailing boats.

Generally the Suffolk landscape ranges from the chalk downlands near the horse racing center of Newmarket, to the forested areas around Brandon on the Suffolk-Norfolk border and the agricultural region of the county associated with the paintings of the archetypal English artist John Constable. Essex, like other parts of East Anglia, still has surprisingly large tracts of farmland and woods despite that fact that in recent years it has become 'commuter land' with many of its inhabitants traveling every day by rail and automobile into the capital city of London to work. Near the Thames estuary it also has some atmospheric salt marshes that are a haven for wildlife. These are currently under threat from the proposed plans to build a third London airport.

In medieval times East Anglia was comparatively one of the most densely populated areas of England. Commercially it was also a wealthy region because of the export of large quantities of wool to continental Europe. In the 14th century this lucrative trade received a boost when a wave of Flemish immigrants who were weavers arrived. The wealth created by the wool industry was reflected in the many grand country houses and large churches that were built in the area during the Middle Ages and the expansion of the existing towns and ports.

There are strong historical connections between East Anglia and the United States. Many of the early Puritan colonists who settled in New England came from the East Anglian area. In the Second World War when America joined Britain in her fight against Nazism several air bases were constructed by the USAF and used to launch bombing raids on Germany and occupied Europe. One base in Norfolk occupied by the British Royal Air Force during the war became an international airport in the 1950s.

When the Roman Catholic missionary Augustine landed in Kent in south-east England in 601 CE he carried a letter from Pope Gregory containing instructions on how to deal with the native heathen Anglo-Saxons. The papal missive told Augustine not to destroy the pagan temples he found, which was the common practice in continental Europe where missionaries like Martin of Tours burnt down the *nemeton* or sacred druidic groves. Instead the pope said they should be 'purified from devil worship [sic] and dedicated to the worship of the true [Christian] God.' This policy is why in East Anglia, as in other parts of the British Isles, churches were built on the sites of pagan shrines or in the vicinity of standing stones that were once objects of veneration in prehistoric times. As late as the 10th and 11th centuries Anglo-Saxon laws were enacted against people still worshipping stones and trees.

At Alphamstane in north Essex there are several interesting looking stones scattered around the hilltop church. One is actually built into the west wall of the nave. Archaeological evidence indicates the site of the church has been occupied since the Bronze Age and Glyn Morgan suggested the stones may be the remnants of a prehistoric megalithic circle. (1982:29). Similar 'pagan stones' can be found in the county at Magdalen Laver, Beauchamp Roding, North Stifford, Fyfield, North Weald, Chadwell St Mary and Ingatestone.

At Ingatestone near Chelmsford one of the stones that gives the village its name, as it is Saxon for 'people of the stone', stands near the south wall of the nave. Originally it was found buried beneath masonry under the church floor. St Botolph's, situated on a prominent hill at Beauchamp Roding, also has a prehistoric standing stone in its churchyard. Local folklore says that when it was decided to build the church the stone was removed and relocated to the bottom of the hill.

The next morning it had been replaced in its original position. After this happened several times the builders decided to leave it *in situ* (Ibid:31). St Botolph is the patron saint of gates and gateways and that may be significant to the local folklore and the legend about the stone. Usually when such events happen they are blamed in folk tradition either on mischievous faeries or the machinations of the Devil who do not want the church built.

Although Anglo-Saxon kings had passed laws to outlaw the practice of *wiccaecrafte* and consulting witches, the first recorded reference to witchcraft in East Anglia was after the Norman Conquest. In 1066 King William of Normandy and his knights defeated the Anglo-Saxon king Harold at the Battle of Hastings in Sussex and conquered England. Despite what some history books say, not all the English submitted meekly to their new masters. For several years after their invasion the Normans were forced to deal with an organized English resistance movement led by patriots such as Earl Edric in Shropshire on the Welsh Border and Hereward the Wake in East Anglia. These rebels were popularly known as the *silvatici* or 'wild men' referring to the fact that they hid in the woods and forests from their enemies and only ventured out to attack them using guerrilla tactics. For that reason Earl Edric in Shropshire was known as 'Edric Silvaticus' or 'Edric the Wild'. It was a tradition that was taken up by medieval outlaws such as Robin Hood, who hid with his Merry Men from the Sheriff of Nottingham in the greenwood of Sherwood Forest.

The primary source for the story of the English rebellion led by Hereward the Wake in East Anglia was *De Gestis Herewardi Saxoni* or *The Life and Deeds of Hereward the Saxon*. This was written about the middle of the 12th century, a hundred years after the event, but was supposed to have been based on contemporary accounts. Hereward was the eldest son of a Saxon noble called Leofric holding land at Bourne in what is now south Lincolnshire. His mother, Lady Ediva, was the descendant of a Northumbrian aristocrat and his father had the title of Earl of Mercia granted to him by Cnut. When the king died Earl Leofric unsuccessfully championed the cause of Cnut's illegitimate son Harald Harefoot as the successor to the English throne.

According to the account given in *De Gestis Herewardi Saxoni*, Hereward was a troublemaker as a teenager who got into fights with his peers and spent his father's money carelessly. As a result Earl Leofric banished his son and at the young age of eighteen he was declared a 'wolfshead' or outlaw. Hereward traveled at first to the Scottish border to stay with his Flemish godfather Gilbert of Ghent. He then lived in Cornwall and Ireland before taking up work as a mercenary fighting in Flanders. Hereward then got married and his wife, Torfrida, was described as a 'wise woman' skilled in the magical arts and astrology.

Although Hereward's father died in 1057 it was several years after the Norman Conquest before he decided to return home and visit his widowed mother. When he arrived at Bourne Hall he found it had been attacked, looted and occupied by the Normans. His younger brother, who had inherited the house and estate in Hereward's absence abroad, had been killed in the raid. His severed head had been placed by the Normans above the gateway to the manor house as a warning to anyone who dared resist them. When Hereward arrived at the house he found a drunken party in progress. He soon ended the revels with his broadsword and battleaxe and the Normans' heads replaced his brother's above the gate.

Hereward was declared an outlaw for this act and he then proceeded to form a small group of resistance fighters by recruiting local men. They took an oath of allegiance to the cause of overthrowing the Norman usurpers at the tomb of St Etheldreda at Ely. The rebel band soon increased in numbers as word spread and to provide himself with legitimacy as their leader Hereward persuaded the Abbot of Peterborough to give him a knighthood. Unfortunately when the sympathetic abbot died King William replaced him with a Norman bishop called Turold. He was a sadistic thug who carried a heavy ceremonial mace or club to smash in his enemies' heads. Hereward joined forces with an invading army of Danes led by one of King Cnut's sons, Sweyn, the king of Denmark. The Saxons and Danes attacked Peterborough, looted the treasure of gold, silver and jewels hoarded by the corrupt monks from the abbey and burnt the town to the ground. They then retreated to their safe refuge in the fens around the Isle of Ely.

King William I, or William the Conqueror as he is popularly known, took the threat of the English rebellion seriously. In 1071 he decided to personally lead the military campaign against Hereward and his rebels. From their fortified stronghold near Ely the English warriors had harried the Norman army as far afield as Norwich in Norfolk and Bury St Edmunds in Suffolk, where the king and saint had been laid to rest. The rebels were in a good position as they were self-sufficient in game, fish and medicinal plants and their local knowledge of the waterways

and the weather aided their 'hit and run' raids against the Norman occupation forces. They were also aided by local people who had no love
for foreign troops. Wearing chainmail and heavily armed with broad-
swords, spears and Viking battleaxes, Hereward and his brave men were
more than a match for the Norman archers and horse-riding knights.

William ordered the building of a causeway across the marshy
ground of the fens using wooden beams, tree trunks and stones so his
troops could travel into the area where the rebels were hiding. Four
wooden siege towers were also built on which were placed *ballistae*
or 'engines', large catapults capable of hurling fireballs or boulders to
bombard the rebel forces. Unfortunately for the Normans, Hereward
heard about this building work and the rebel army destroyed the causeway and its towers. It has been suggested that the Norman king wanted
to make peace with the outlaw but was overruled by his nobles. They
insisted that if the occupation was to be a success and long-lasting the
English had to be forced to fear their new lords and so any rebels had
to be slaughtered without mercy.

The king knew he could not defeat Hereward the Wake using military might alone as his native rebel army had the advantage. Desperate times called for desperate measures and William was persuaded to
try supernatural methods to try and overcome his arch-enemy. Victor
Heard (1995) says: 'For centuries the Fens were regarded with superstitious fear as a province of magic and mystery, and as Christianity sup-
planted paganism they retained this special quality'. William's hench-
man Ivo Taillebois, who was widely reviled for torturing and harassing
his English tenants and seems to have had a personal vendetta against
Hereward, told the king he knew a witch who could help them. She
would use her powers to create fear and havoc among the superstitious
English rebels and allow the Normans to defeat them. At first William
was reluctant to get involved in such dark arts, but his lack of military
success against Hereward overcame his objections. It is said that the
witch was French and was brought over from France especially for the
task of defeating the English rebellion.

Meanwhile, the rebels had heard rumors from their local contacts
that the Normans were planning 'something evil' against them. It was
decided that a spy would be sent to Brandedon or Brandon, where the
Norman army had its headquarters, to find out what was going on.
When nobody was willing to volunteer for the mission Hereward said
he would go. He cut short his aristocratically long hair, shaved his beard

off and threw on a tattered cloak. The rebel leader entered the town disguised as a traveling potter selling his wares and sought lodgings at a widow's house. Coincidentally, and unbeknown to Hereward, the witch who had been employed by the Normans was also staying as a guest at the house.

Hereward heard the widow and her guest conversing in French. Obviously not thinking that the lodger could understand the language, they were discussing how the rebel forces would be overcome by magical powers and defeated. In the middle of the night the two women left the house and went to a spring in the garden. Hereward followed them at a distance and overheard them asking the spirit guardian of the spring questions and listening attentively for the answers. Although Hereward was briefly captured by the Normans when he recklessly entered the king's quarters, he managed to escape and returned to the fens with the intelligence about the witch's plan.

King William built a new causeway and siege towers and, according to the ancient *Chronicle of Croyland Abbey*, the *pythonissa* or sorceress was raised up by ropes to the top of one of the wooden towers on the causeway. She was protected by Norman archers standing at the base of the tower with crossbows. From this high vantage point the witch was able to cast her spells and curses to call down destruction on the rebels. Having been forewarned, several of the Saxons crept up to the base of the wooden tower. They overcame her bodyguards and as the witch began her incantations for the third and final time used bundles of dry reeds to set it alight. The fire quickly spread from the blazing tower along the wooden causeway and the Norman soldiers fled in panic. Those who were not burnt to death in the flames or drowned in the marsh were cut down by the rebels. The witch is said to have died when she fell from the tower to escape the flames and broke her neck.

E. W. Liddell, a hereditary initiate of the Pickingill Craft, has claimed, without offering any historical evidence, that the 'witch of Brandon' was called Julia Pickingill and belonged to an infamous East Anglian witch family. Allegedly, its most famous descendant was the 19th century cunning man George Pickingill of Canewdon in Essex who will be discussed later in this book. Julia was allegedly branded as a traitor by the Pickingill clan because she had helped the Normans by leading them along the secret paths in the fens that were known to local witches. However, Liddell claims, Hereward the Wake knew the witches had 'placed the runes' on the traitor to bring about her death. Because of this knowledge the rebels were no longer frightened of the witch's powers. They knew they were fated to be, quite literally, the agents of her downfall (Liddell 1994:34).

Interestingly in his work *Germania* the Roman historian Tacitus mentioned a famous seer called Veleda who belonged to the Bructei tribe in the Rhineland. According to Tacitus, the seer was widely consulted, even by Roman generals. She sat atop a 'high tower' when obtaining her visions of the future and her relatives then carried the messages of the spirits to the Roman army. Similarly 'raised platforms' were used for prophecy, trance and spells by the ancient Norse seers known as *volvas* who were priestesses of the goddess Freya. Many writers regard them as prototypes of later medieval witches.

Eventually Hereward the Wake was betrayed by the monks at Ely and in October 1071 his fenland stronghold was overwhelmed by the Normans. He and most of his rebels managed to escape using their knowledge of the secret routes though the marshes provided by the local witches. They carried on their resistance to Norman rule in the Forest of Brunesweald on the border between Cambridgeshire and Northamptonshire. In 1073 Hereward finally gave up his campaign and he sued for peace with William. He and his men were granted pardons by the king and the English rebel regained his stolen lands and died peacefully in old age.

Richard Deacon has said that, despite its closeness to London, the county of Essex retained its ancient Saxon heritage. Because of this it 'has preserved in its folklore many pagan customs, including the appeasing of the fairies by putting bowl of oatmeal out for them at night. Such customs were maintained until quite recent years (and may even be kept up today) in the lonely salt marshes and the creeks...' (Deacon 1976:51). Of course today country people say they are putting out bowls of bread and milk at night 'for the hedgehogs.'

Writing in the 1960s the amateur folklorist Eric Maple coined the term 'witch country' to describe Essex, and especially the marshy land near the Thames estuary close to villages renowned for witchcraft such as Canewdon. Referring to the county a local writer said: 'Three centuries ago the villages were smaller and more isolated, the villagers less educated and more superstitious than their modern counterparts. Their feelings and reactions to natural phenomena can still be sensed by those visiting one of the more isolated hamlets set among the low-lying mudflats along the east coast of that county.' (Morgan 1982). In fact Eric

Maple's description of 'witch country' could just as easily be used to describe the whole region of East Anglia.

Most of eastern England was under 'Danelaw' for several centuries before the Norman Conquest and several foreign influences impacted on the evolution and development of witch beliefs and practices in the area. E.W. Liddell has claimed that historical witchcraft in East Anglia was heavily influenced by the Danes and their Scandinavian pagan religion and also by the medieval Flemish weavers, who he says brought with them French witch beliefs and the Cathar heresy. Folklorist and writer Nigel Pennick, who lives in Cambridge and is a follower of the 'Nameless Art' (witchcraft) of East Anglian, has claimed that in the 17th century during the English civil war Scottish prisoners-of-war were transported to the Cambridgeshire fens. There they were used as slave labor on local drainage projects converting the marshes into farmland. Pennick claims some of these POWs were witches and their magical techniques were incorporated into the local East Anglian folk magic. He also says that in the 1840s Irish immigrants escaping the potato famine in their homeland settled in East Anglia. They allegedly introduced elements of the old Celtic faery faith into witchcraft that was prevalent in the area (Pennick 1995:42).

When the prosecution of alleged witches began eastern England was certainly an area that was renowned for the practice of witchcraft. In 1618 the Cambridge theologian William Perkins said that the common people in the rural districts around the university city 'revered and honoured' the cunning folk. In fact he said they thought themselves 'blessed' to have so many living in the county. This was because in the days before proper doctors and a state-run health service sick people often went to cunning folk and 'white witches' to be cured. Writing in the previous century about popular superstition, the philosopher Sir Thomas More claimed that 'many fools' had more faith in 'wise witches' than they had in the Church or in God. In fact he said one contemporary 'wise man' who was widely consulted by the 'ignorant peasants' was known as 'the god of Norfolk'.

Sir James Howell, the historiographer royal in the court of King Charles II (reigned 1649–1685), wrote in a letter to a friend in Paris: 'We have multitudes of witches amongst us, for in Essex and Suffolk alone there were about two hundred indicted within two years and about a half of them executed'. In his research into historical cunning folk and witches in Essex from 1560 to 1580, Alan Macfarlane discovered the surviving court records contained references to at least sixty male and female witches. Based on the statistics for 1560–1603 Macfarlane estimated that no villager in Essex was more than ten miles away from a witch or cunning person (1991:117–118).

The historian Professor Owen Davies, who has made a comprehensive study of historical cunning folk and witches in England, says they were often self-employed artisans and trades people. He claims that the laboring class, who in East Anglian would have been mostly employed in farming, were far too busy with their daily tasks from dawn to dusk to be cunning folk. In contrast self-employed artisans, shop owners and tradespeople had more time and could receive clients at their places of work. If they had to make house calls then their assistants or apprentices could run the business while they were absent. Few of the cunning folk however made enough money solely from their magical work to do it as a fulltime profession. In the majority of cases they worked part-time and had other jobs that supplied their main income (Davies 2009:69).

As regards the gender of English cunning folk and witches, the idea is often put forward that in historical times practitioners of witchcraft were exclusively women. This provides support for the modern feminist concept that the witch-hunts were fuelled by misogyny and were a patriarchal conspiracy against womankind. This was not true and in East Anglia the statistics show that while 90% of alleged witches were female 10% were actually male. The gender of victims of bewitchment was even closer being 54% women and 46% men.

Likewise the witnesses in court cases involving allegations of witchcraft were 48% female. Women obviously had no qualms in accusing others of their gender and there was no feminist type sisterhood. Historian Keith Thomas has said that 'the idea that witch-persecutions reflected a war between the sexes must be discounted, not least because the victims and witnesses were themselves as likely to be women then men.' (1991:568). In reference to accusations of witchcraft in East Anglia, Alan Macfarlane agreed: 'There is no evidence that hostility between the sexes lay behind the prosecutions. Essex pamphlets [about witch trials] show women witnessing as often as men against other women.' (1970:160). Thomas and Macfarlane both confirm that there are many East Anglian examples of women accusing women of practicing witchcraft and casting malefic spells. In the period when the death penalty was in place for witchcraft this could have led to the accused being hanged.

There is also evidence of social tensions involving family or neighborhood feuds or disagreements resulting in accusations of witchcraft. In 1623 for example a shopkeeper in Ipswich in Suffolk called Thomas Methwolde married the widow of an apothecary. Unfortunately the marital relationship did not go smoothly. It seems that the family of Methwolde's new wife objected to the marriage and tried their best to break it up. As a result the shop owner appears to have resorted to witchcraft to stop them as he appeared in court charged with bewitching his wife's niece.

A feud between two families in Norfolk, the Stockdales and the Cremers, also led to accusations of witchcraft. In 1600 Nicholas Stockdale was brought before the magistrates for allegedly bewitching a flock of sheep belonging to the Cremers. The charge was withdrawn after it was discovered that the illness the animals were suffering from had been caused by overeating. The Cremers had put the sheep into a field containing freshly cut barley and the animals over-indulged themselves on the crop. However two years later the Cremers again accused Stockdale and this time it was of bewitching people who had died in mysterious circumstances. It was a charge that could have been punishable by the death penalty. He was acquitted again and the court awarded him compensation of 40 pounds sterling in damages for the defamation of his reputation. That was a lot of money in those days.

Another feud between neighbors that ended up in court took place in Cambridge and involved Margaret Cotton and a Dorcas Swetton. It broke out after a legal dispute between the two women about the right to sit in a particular pew in church. Cotton lost the case and was forced to pay Swetton several pounds in legal costs. Swetton then accused her of bewitching her baby to death and in 1603 Margaret Cotton was brought to trial. She was acquitted on that occasion but then appeared before the magistrates again six years later. This time she was charged with bewitching three people. The prosecution's case collapsed when the witnesses admitted they had been paid by the Swetton family to lie in court. (Biggs 1997:366).

Common terms used in the historical period in East Anglia, as elsewhere, to describe practitioners of the magical arts variously included cunning man, wise woman, white witch, black witch, gray witch, wizard, sorcerer, conjuror (somebody who conjured or summoned up spirits), blesser (healer), hedge doctor (a man or woman who used herbs and plants for healing), diviner, enchanter, charmer, planet-reader (astrologer), herb man and herb woman, and soothsayer (fortune-teller). Emma Wilby has said that in common parlance the same folk magical practitioner could be called a 'witch' by one person, a 'wise woman' or 'wise man' by another and a 'conjuror' by somebody else (2005:26). These descriptions seemed to have been interchangeable and were used by both ordinary people who consulted these magical practitioners and by the Church who condemned them.

The definition of a witch seems to have been fairly consistent over the centuries when witchcraft was a crime and its practitioners were prosecuted. In his book *A Discourse Concerning the Subtle Practices of Devils* (1587), the Essex preacher George Gifford defined the witch as follows; 'A witch is one who worketh by the Devil or by some curious arte either healing or revealing things secret, or foretelling things to come which the Devil has devised to ensnare men's souls...the conjuror, the enchanter, the sorcerer, the diviner and whatever other sort there is encompassed within this circle.' He added that the common people did not hate and fear witches on religious and theological grounds. Instead they feared the power of witchcraft to cause harm to themselves, their property, livestock and crops. Gifford said it was not because witches were believed to be the secret agents of satanic forces and the 'powers of darkness.'

In 1594 the Essex lawyer William Smith described the witch as 'being deluded by a league [an agreement for mutual protection and assistance] made with the Devil through his persuasion and juggling [trickery and misrepresentation], thinkest she [sic] can design what manner of things so ever...' This 'manner of things' according to Smith included the raising of storms to destroy crops and fruit trees and to be carried to another place by her familiar spirit who took animal form as a pig, calf or goat. Once at this 'another place' Smith said the witch spent the night hours 'playing, sporting, banqueting, dalliance and diverse other devilish lusts and lewd disports...' This was a reference to the so-called Witches Sabbath more usually found in European accounts of witchcraft.

At the height of the East Anglian persecution of suspected witches in 1646 the Reverend John Gaule, the vicar of Great Stoughtonin Huntingdonshire, bravely published an anti-witchcraft tract entitled *Select Cases of Conscience Touching Witches and Witchcraft*. In it he claimed that superstitious and gullible country folk believed a witch to be any 'grey old woman with a wrinkled face, furr'd brow, a hairy lip, a gobber [single] tooth, a squinty eye, a squeaking voice, or a scolding tongue, having a ragged coat on her back, a scullcap on her head, a spindle in her hand, and a dog or cat by her side.' This was a stereotyped and archetypal image that reflected popular beliefs about what a witch physically looked like.

Another East Anglian clergyman, the Reverend Samuel Harsnett from Colchester in Essex, also described the physical characteristics people believed identified someone as a witch. He described a typical witch as 'an old and weather-beaten crone having her chin and her knees meeting with age, hollow-eyed, untoothed, furrowed in the face, having her lips trembling with the palsy, going mumbling in the streets; one that hath forgotten the paternoster [the Lord's Prayer] and hath yet a shrewd tongue in her head to call a drab [prostitute] a drab.' Harsnett became famous for his exposure of charlatans, knaves, rogues and mountebanks who pretended to have magical powers or psychic abilities and he ended his clerical career as the Archbishop of York. Whether these exaggerated images bordering on caricature were based on any truth or not, it is how ordinary people imagined witches. In reality, as has been seen, they could be both men and women and were of all ages.

William Perkins, mentioned earlier, was a Fellow of Christ's College, Cambridge from 1584 to 1594 and was described by his contemporaries as an 'uncompromising Puritan minister'. Perkins seems to have been overly obsessed with witches and witchcraft. He preached numerous 'hellfire and brimstone' sermons from the pulpit of churches in the city condemning the 'damnable arte' and its many practitioners in the city and surrounding countryside. After his death in 1602 these sermons were collected together and published for the edification of the masses in a cheap fifty-four-page pamphlet called *A Discourse of the Damned Arte of Witchcraft*.

In one of his sermons delivered at St Andrew's church in Cambridge the clergyman claimed that he knew of contemporary witches who had made a pact with the Devil. He compared them unfavorably with the ancient 'enchanters of Egypt' and the sorcerer Simon Magus (Simon the Magician) who was at one time a rival to Jesus. In his sermons the Reverend Perkins claimed that the witches were 'aged persons of weak brains and troubled with an abundance of melancholy.' For that reason they were easy prey for the Devil who took advantage of them. However, paradoxically, the misogynistic Perkins also said the witch was 'wise and clever, yea as crafty and cunning in all matters.' He had observed that the female sex was naturally weaker and more nervous then men. Therefore they were more easily 'entangled in the Devil's illusions.'

William Perkins (1558–1602), author of *A Discourse of the Damned Arte of Witchcraft.*

Generally witches were popularly and widely regarded as anti-social, destructive and evil people. They were believed to be usually old unmarried or widowed women who went around begging alms and gossips who possessed vicious tempers and tongues. They were ill-natured, spiteful, malicious and of a wicked disposition. This reflected the prevailing attitude to those who were on the fringes of society or were different in any way and regarded as outsiders or deviants from the norm.

In the accusations made against one group of suspected witches in Essex, four of the women involved were either unmarried, single mothers with illegitimate children or had challenged moral values by becoming pregnant before marriage. One alleged witch was suspected of having committed incest with her son, one had quarreled many times with her husband and would not be obedient to him, one had been overheard reciting prayers in the forbidden language of Latin (associated with the Roman Church) and two others were well-known as a 'lewd woman' and an 'old whore.' Therefore accusations of witchcraft were often made against social outsiders who their contemporaries regarded as dysfunctional breakers of the prevailing moral code and challengers of normal conventions.

When considering accusations of witchcraft theologians and judges alike did not seem to have thought there was any difference between so-called 'black' witches and 'white' witches or between the witches and cunning folk. Again this remained a firm and constant view throughout the period of the witch-hunts. The Ecclesiastical Commission of 1559 for instance condemned both the practice of operative witchcraft, defined widely as the use of sorcery, charms, incantations, casting magical circles, soothsaying and summoning and communicating with spirits, and also people who consulted cunning folk and witches for their advice and help.

In 1582 when Ursula Kemp of Chelmsford was accused of practicing 'black witchcraft' it was said she was formerly a 'white witch.' In court Kemp protested her innocence and claimed she did not 'witch', only 'unwitch', i.e., take bewitchments and spells off people and remove curses. Ten years earlier Margery Skelton had been prosecuted in a secular court as a well known 'black witch'. Ironically in 1566 she had previously appeared before a church court for practicing as a 'blessing witch' or 'white witch' (Macfarlane 1970:128). John Stearne, the notorious assistant to the 17th century Witchfinder-General Matthew Hopkins, described 'white witches' as 'silly, ignorant people whose eyes are blinded by Satan.'

The Cambridge theologian William Perkins said that 'by witches we understand not only those who kill and torment, but all diviners,

charmers, jugglers [conjurors or spirit evokers], all wizards commonly called wise men, and wise women' (quoted in Davies 2003:15). He
claimed that a cunning person or witch could only heal somebody because they had been possessed by the Devil and the healer had made a
pact with the Old One. In the 1640s a pamphlet was issued called *Lawes
Against Witches and Conjuration* that stated that wizards and magicians
were just as guilty of 'damnable crime' as those who practiced witchcraft. The anonymous writer of the pamphlet said that the wizard and
the conjuror still used 'superstitious and ceremonial forms or words
(called 'charmes'), medicines, herbes and other things'. Also when they
'divined things to come' it was still carried out like the witches did, with
the help of the Devil through a covenant or pact they had made with
him (ibid:9).

In the 17th century the Reverend John Gaule expressed his considered opinion that the so-called 'good witch' was in fact the worst and
most wicked type. His reasoning was that the so-called white witches
only pretended to do good works in the name of God. In reality they
were secretly the servants of the Devil. John Stearne, mentioned earlier,
did recognize that there could be good and bad witches. However he
added that in practice it did not really matter as all witches were in
league with the Devil and were to be hunted down and killed (ibid:30).

Although the majority of clergy in East Anglia were anti-witchcraft
a few seem to have had a more enlightened view. For instance in 1602
Thomas Veare of Horndon-on-Hill in Essex appeared before a church
court on a charge of slander. He had been telling people that a carpenter
in the village had traveled to London to consult a cunning woman about
a stolen piece of female underwear. Apparently the story was untrue (or
so the man claimed) and the court made Veare apologize and do penance for the sin of telling a lie.

In 1656 the Reverend Ralph Josselin, the minister at Earls Colne in
Essex) intervened when one of his parishioners called Biford was accused of being a notorious 'he-witch' (sic). A 'gentleman of the parish'
(i.e., a wealthy homeowner or landowner) had claimed that the alleged
witch had cursed his child and as a result the villagers turned against
him. The Reverend Josselin took the accused man for a walk in the fields
and discussed the matter with him. As a result of this conversation the
minister concluded that 'the poor wretch is innocent to that evil' and
should be left alone.

The following year the clergyman was involved in another accusation of witchcraft in the neighboring parish of Gaines Colne. The Reverend Josselin was told by its minister that one of his flock, Ann Crow, had been labeled a witch by her neighbors. She had been seen acting in a suspicious manner in the churchyard near a grave that was not one of her family. Also a strange animal 'like a rat, only reddish in colour and with no tail' had been seen scampering about near her. The superstitious villagers believed this was a familiar spirit given to her by the Devil. After questioning the old woman Josselin declared publicly she was innocent and no further action was taken against her by the villagers (Sharpe 1991:242).

Although the witch or cunning person was supposed to be widely feared by the general population and faced persecution and prosecution, they seem to have brazenly adopted a social costume or eccentric way of dressing. This singled them out from ordinary folk and indicated their special calling and powers. Female practitioners of the magical art in East Anglia often wore a red cap, hence the generic name for a witch in East Anglia 'Old Mother Redcap', or a red skirt or red cloak. Around their necks they would wear several polecat or weasel skins joined and stitched together to form a collar. Special belts made of knotted horsehair or eel skins and colored scarves were worn around the waist to keep skirts and trousers in place. Often a witch or cunning person would wear an item of clothing inside out or have odd socks or stockings so that people would know what they were (Pennick 1995:102–103). Elaborate garters, such as those made of fox, eel or snakeskin, were also worn as a hidden symbol that the wearer belonged to the witch-cult.

Pre-Christian magical practitioners had often worn a special ritual costume and this can be seen as the pagan Scandinavian influence on East Anglia and its witch beliefs. The *volvas* or Norse seers and sorceresses who were priestesses of the witch-goddess Freya mentioned earlier were one example. They wore a dark blue cloak with a hood decorated with semi-precious stones around the hem. It had an inner hood or cap made from the fur of a lynx, a fox or a badger and the sorceress also wore gloves and boots made from cat skin. They also carried a special staff or wand made of iron with a knob on the end. One of these was recently identified as such an object in the collection of the British Museum that is not on public display. It had been unearthed from a 10th century grave in Scandinavia and the end had been bent, probably to negate its power now that its owner had passed to the spirit world or to prevent her becoming a 'night walker' or restless ghost who haunted the living (*The Times* December 31st 2013).

How did people in East Anglia become witches? Theologians and clerics obviously believed it was through making an infernal pact with the Devil in exchange for supernatural powers. As far as the clergy were concerned this was a fact and it was confirmed for them by the testimony given by suspected witches and witnesses in court cases. Often this testimony was freely given without any form of torture or coercion. In 1645 the Suffolk witch Anne Harner confessed that the Devil had come to her 'in the likeness of a black man.' A Huntingdonshire woman called Jane Wallis indicted a year later claimed Old Nick manifested to her as 'a man in black cloathes.' He had 'ugly feete' (cloven?) and could change shape at will, sometimes appearing as a tall man and other times as a small one before vanishing completely into thin air (Davenport 1616:12). In 1616 Mary Smith of King's Lynn in Norfolk said the Devil also came to her in the form of a 'black man.' He spoke to Smith in a 'low, mumbling and hissing voice' that frightened her.

The author of *Antidote to Atheism* (1590) Dr Henry More, a Cambridge scholar and Fellow of Christ's College, said he personally believed in witchcraft because he had met people who had been initiated into the cult. One told Dr More she had been introduced to a prospective husband by a Mrs Lendall who was later hanged in the city as a witch. The young woman told the scholar she was invited for supper one evening by Mrs Lendall. The other guests who were present included a mysterious and sinister 'man dressed in black' who all the others, who she now suspected to be witches, bowed to in reverence before the meal commenced.

In the 1640s Rebecca Jones first met a man she suspected was the Devil when she was a servant in the house of John Bishop of Great Clacton in Essex. One day there was a knock at the door and when she opened it there stood a tall, dark and handsome young man. Evidently he was the Devil in disguise and she dedicated herself to his service from that day on (Ewen 1933:273). A similar story was told by a witch from Great Yarmouth, Suffolk. One night she also heard knocking at the door. When she opened it a 'tall dark man' was standing outside illuminated in the moonlight. He asked to look at her hand and then, producing a knife from under his cloak, cut it, drawing blood. The witch said that the 'dark man' told her that now she belonged to him 'body and soul.' Apparently the scar from the wound never faded and had stayed with her ever since.

When people were suspected of witchcraft, especially women, the witch-hunters would strip them naked, shave off their body hair and search for the *Diablo stigmata* or 'Devil's Mark' given to them at their initiation. This could either be a small tattoo in the form of a spider or a bat or a blue or black spot on the skin. In practice however any wart, birthmark, scar or skin blemish was taken by the witchfinders as evidence of the Mark. The Cambridgeshire justice of the peace, Michael Dalton, even said that it could resemble a flea bite. In the unhygienic conditions prevalent in the 16th and 17th centuries few people would have been without an insect bite or some form of skin infection so it made the witchfinders' task a lot easier.

In some cases when they entered the witch-cult the candidate seems to have taken part in some kind of sexual induction or 'marriage' with the 'Man in Black', who was probably the local human representative of the Horned One. A Suffolk witch, Ellen Driver, confessed in 1645 that the Devil had appeared to her as an ordinary man except that he had cloven feet. He persuaded her to renounce God and the authority of the Church and marry him. Driver claimed that from then on the Devil visited her on a regular basis and they frequently had sexual relations. As a result the woman claimed she had borne her demon lover two children who she described as 'changelings' (Hole 1977:45). An Essex witch, Rebecca West, told her accusers that the Devil materialized in her bedroom in the middle of the night. She was unable to refuse his advances and after they had made love several times Old Nick said he would be her husband until the day she died (Howell 1816:842).

A form of solitary initiation into the witch-cult was reported from the Isle of Ely in the 1640s. It was a local belief that if a person wanted to become a witch all they had to do was to secret the host in their mouth during communion. After they had drunk the communion wine the would-be witch then went outside and urinated against the church wall. He or she then sought out a toad and fed the stolen host to it. From that time on they could consider themselves to be a witch. A similar folk ritual is also found in the witch lore of both Wales and the south-west of England.

Sometimes new witches were introduced to the cult by relatives who were already members. In 1566 an Essex witch, Elizabeth Francis, said she been taught witchcraft by her aged grandmother. The old woman had told her to renounce the false Christian God and the Bible. Instead she had to 'give her blood to the Devil' (Rosen 1991:73–74). Twenty-three years later another witch from Essex called Joan Curry said she had been taught witchcraft by an older woman called Mother Humphrey. She told Curry make a circle on the ground. She then had to kneel down and pray to the 'chief of the devils' and spirits would appear who would help her. Curry did as she was told and three spirits duly appeared in the form of white, gray and black colored imps.

Dr Mark Taylor, who was a general practitioner, tells a modern story of a noted male charmer in a Norfolk village at the beginning of the 20th century who knew he was dying. He had no close relatives to whom he could pass on his power so he sent for the minister's daughter. She had to swear not to reveal the secret of his charming power to anyone but her own chosen successor. She apparently kept the secret all her life and performed very well as the old charmer's replacement (Taylor 1929:117).

Sometimes those witches and cunning folk who were literate obtained some of their knowledge from books on the occult sciences and magical arts. In 1687 Ann Watts, a fortune-teller who usually followed her trade in London, was discovered sleeping rough in a wood on the country estate of Sir William Holcroft in Essex. She regularly visited the county seeking new clients and not wanting to pay for lodgings often slept under the stars. Watts was arrested for vagrancy and brought before the magistrates for sentencing. Several 'magical books' were found in her possession including a copy of Agrippa's *Occult Philosophy*, Reginald Scot's *Discoverie of Witchcraft* (an anti-witchcraft book that was nevertheless highly prized by cunning folk and witches because it contained many spells and charms) and an astrological almanac. All the books were confiscated by order of the court and burnt (Sharpe 1996:281).

A famous Cambridgeshire practitioner of the Old Craft was known as 'Daddy Witch,' even though she was female. East Anglian folklorist Nigel Pennick has suggested that 'Daddy' was a nickname among rural people for the horned god of the witches (1995:5). The witch lived in a tumbledown cottage encircled by water like a moat that was later known as 'Daddy Witch's Pond.' Her occult knowledge was supposed to have come from a magical book of unknown provenance she owned called *The Devil's Plantation*. Possibly it was one of the handwritten 'black books' of spells, charms and conjurations known to be owned by witches and cunning folk and often passed down through families. Unfortunately the book did not survive the witch's death and its exact contents and their provenance are unknown.

In the English witch trials those prosecuted were not regarded as heretics as they were in European countries. The alleged witches were charged with *maleficium* or practicing malefic magic to cause harm to humans, livestock and crops rather than indulging in heretical or anti-Christian activities and orgiastic orgies of devil-worship. Because accounts of such activities were not mentioned in the court records does not mean they did not take place in the English countryside. They may not have been recorded in the trials because they were not regarded as important in relation to the central charges of causing harm or the court officials did not ask the right questions. However there are a few tantalizing references that suggest the 'Witches' Sabbath' was sometimes practised by historical witches in East Anglia.

In 1643 for instance several men and women appeared in court at Chelmsford (Essex) charged with practicing the interesting combination of 'conjuration, magic and lechery.' The chief witness was a servant woman, Martha Hurrell, and she claimed that during the period between Easter and Michaelmas (September 29th) of 1643 she and a group of other people met regularly together in various country houses to practice magic. In her disposition Hurrell named the others involved as Robert and Thomas Aylett, James Richardson, John Deir, Lambert Smith, Ellen Warren, William Drake and his wife (unnamed), 'all of Stinsted [Stansted?]', three male servants and two maids from the household of Sir William Maxie, Edward Motting of Bocking, two women called Sarah Fletcher and Elizabeth Waite, and a 'conjuror' or summoner of spirits described as a man 'in black apparel with brown hair and a blackish beard.'

During the period mentioned Hurrell said she attended three meetings at her master's house, 'half a score' (ten) at the houses of William Drake and at Lady Eden's and Sir Robert Lumley's houses once or twice. These meetings were always held at night and when they met at the house where Hurrell worked and lived they 'took Mistress Drurie out of her bed'. (Drurie's name is not mentioned in the previous paragraph's list of consorts.) She was carried into the hall where the conjuror and other men 'had the use of her body.' Martha Hurrell's husband was also present at these gatherings and Elizabeth Waite and Sarah Fletcher pulled up his shirt and kissed him. They then 'took up their coats' and both women lay on top of him and said afterwards that 'he did them some good.' Hurrell also described how the servants who worked for Sir William Maxie conjured up spirits. They did this by drawing a circle on the floor in their master's hall and burning three candles. The group feasted afterwards and danced to the music of a fiddler and Hurrell told the court 'all of high and low order mingled together.' (Haining 1974:137–138). This concept of witch coven with a membership drawn from a wide range of social ranks features in many historical accounts of witchcraft and has survived today.

Cambridgeshire witches were also supposed to gather in groups and meet at night in the fields around the village of Horseheath. Many eyewitnesses claimed to have seen them 'frolicking and dancing' and claimed people returning from these revels in the early hours were exhausted and in a 'terrible state of perspiration' (Pennick 1995:52). In her *Notes on Cambridgeshire Witchcraft* (1915), Catherine Parsons said that the famous Daddy Witch was one of 'many witches and wizards who flocked around Horseheath to attend the frolics and dances held at midnight in lonely fields by the Master Witch of the neighbourhood.' This 'Master Witch' would have been the local 'Man in Black' or the human representative of the Devil or Horned God. It was also said that in the 19th century Horseheath Fair was often frequented by one of these local witches and she 'danced the hornpipe [dance] better than any man or woman for miles around'. Every man, young or old, was eager to dance with her.

In 1850 a millwright from the Cambridgeshire Fens had to repair the broken machinery at an isolated windmill on a river bank near Prickwillow. Because it was a major job and some distance from his home, the man spent a week sleeping in the loft of a derelict cottage on the riverside. One night he was awakened by the sound of voices coming from downstairs. He cautiously peered down through the half-open trapdoor of the loft into the sitting room of the cottage below. He saw two women lighting a fire in the hearth using pieces of wood he had discarded from his repair work that day.

As the millwright watched from his hiding place four more women entered the cottage. One he recognized as an inhabitant of the village where he lived. Each of the women was wrapped in a long black cloak and carried a basket made from rushes from which they took bread and cheese and a bottle of ale. They sat in a circle on the floor in front of the blazing fire and as the room warmed up removed their cloaks. Underneath they were almost completely naked. One of the women showed her companions the garters she wore as her only item of clothing that were made from plaited horsehair. Another was also wearing garters made from snakeskin and the witness said these garments had some special significance to the assembled women.

As he watched the strange scene the man accidentally touched the half-open trapdoor and it fell with a loud noise. The women screamed in fright and fled in panic from the cottage. However in their haste to leave one of the women left her cloak behind. When he had finished repairing the mill the man went to the village of Brandon Creek and sought out a woman who was reputed to be a witch. He recognized her as the one in the cottage who had fled leaving her cloak behind. The millwright handed it over and told her how he had found it. The witch responded by spitting in his face. She said if he ever spoke of the matter publicly then as surely as he made his living from windmills they would be the cause of his death. The witch's prophecy came true some time later when the wall of a mill the man was working on collapsed and he was killed by the falling rubble.

When a witch died the disposal of their remains was often a problem. They were sometimes buried in unconsecrated ground or at crossroads. When Daddy Witch of Horseheath passed from this world to the next, the local minister refused permission for her to be interred in the churchyard. Instead she was buried in the middle of the road near her former cottage. It was said that horses and dogs would refuse to pass the spot. In the same village there once lived a witch who said she did not want her recently deceased husband buried in consecrated ground. Eventually she was forced by the authorities to agree to the burial. However on their way to the churchyard the men bearing the coffin had to keep putting it down and rest as it was so heavy. Eventually they became suspicious and opened the casket. Inside there was no body and it was just full of stones. The witch had secretly buried her husband elsewhere as she had wanted to do.

2

The Witch Trials

THE ATTITUDE TO magic by the Church and the political Establishment in the 15th and 16th centuries was largely ambivalent because the ruling power elite and the upper class used magicians, consulted astrologers and employed alchemists. The classic example is Dr John Dee, not only the court astrologer to Queen Elizabeth I (1558–1603) but also a magician who conjured up spirits and communicated with angels. A letter exists written by one of the queen's advisors Lord Burghley to Dr Dee's magical assistant and seer Edward Kelly begging him to return to England and use his alchemical skills to make gold (Rosen 1969:5). Before he met Dr Dee, Kelly and another man called Paul Waring had participated in a necromantic rite in a Lancashire churchyard to call up the spirits of the dead. Some aristocrats also practised witchcraft and magic themselves and this was especially widespread in Scotland.

As magicians and necromancers were accepted in the higher circles of society, or at least a blind eye was turned to their activities if it was politically expedient to do so, before the Tudor period a certain tolerance was shown to magical practitioners in general. Paradoxically most of the early court cases dealing with accusations of witchcraft and sorcery before the 16th century often involved members of the aristocracy and were in the context of political conspiracies and plots against the monarchy and the ruling class.

In legal statutes during the reign of King Henry VIII (reigned 1509–1547) it was stated that' artificers [such] as smiths, weavers, and women boldly and customarily take upon them great cures and things of great difficulty in which they partly use sorcery...' In 1542 King Henry passed a law against witchcraft that only remained in force for a short time before it was repealed by his successor, the young King Edward VI (1547–1553). The law had nothing to do with condemning or punishing heresy or so-called devil worship. Instead its purpose was to curb the activities of treasure-hunters who consulted magicians, witches and diviners and used magical rituals to find hoards in prehistoric burial mounds and ruined churches, abbeys and castles. These magical rituals may have been based on a superstitious belief surviving from pagan times that ancient burial places and treasure hoards were haunted by guardian spirits.

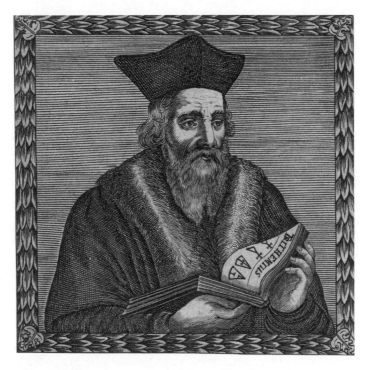

Edward Kelley, engraving from *A Tour in Wales* by
Thomas Pennant, 1781.

Barbara Rosen has suggested that King Henry's witchcraft law was a rare gesture towards Roman Catholics in the sense that it was an attempt to restrict the iconoclastic activities of radical religious reformers. They were known to have joined in the activities of treasure-seek-ers as a cover to loot and destroy church property and artifacts. Rosen adds that, paradoxically, considering the king's stormy relationship with Rome, the magical paraphernalia mentioned and outlawed by the new law, such as crowns, scepters (wands), swords, rings and glasses (mirrors and crystals), also appeared in earlier papal bulls or official proclamations made against witchcraft and sorcery (Rosen 1969:22–23).

In 1560 the bishop of Salisbury (Wiltshire), John Jewell, well-known for his puritan leanings, preached a sermon before Queen Elizabeth I shortly after she came to the throne. In it he said: 'This kind of people, I mean witches and sorcerers, within these last few years are marvellously increased within Your Grace's realm.' He went on to request that the new queen should pass laws against witchcraft because it was the wish and desire of subjects who were allegedly suffering at the hand of these witches. (Hole:1977:12).

A year later in 1561 another bishop wrote to Queen Elizabeth's Secretary of State, Sir William Cecil, and asked that a new law on witchcraft be passed as soon as possible. This letter was written because the Chief Justice of England had informed the worried the bishop that under the existing laws no legal action could be taken against magicians and sorcerers. Despite this claim in 1560 in Essex two people had been accused at the assizes of practicing witchcraft.

Subsequently two years later in 1563 a new Witchcraft Act was placed on the statute books. In many ways it followed the theme and wording of the law put in place by Elizabeth's father King Henry VIII. The new act prohibited the conjuration or summoning of evil spirits for any purpose and those found guilty could face the death penalty. It also banned the use of witchcraft, enchanting, charming and sorcery. These categories of magical practice including bewitching to death, destroying personal goods, property and livestock, seeking treasure or looking for lost things, provoking unlawful love (so-called amatory magic), or using spells and (oral) charms to kill, injure and maim people. Bewitching somebody so they died was punishable by death by hanging and the other practices drew lesser sentences of a combination of imprisonment and sessions in the public pillory where the culprit was physically abused by the mob. If a person repeated the offence then, depending on the seriousness of the crime, they could either face life imprisonment or a death sentence.

Despite Queen Elizabeth's patronage of Dr John Dee, the Witchcraft Act of 1563 also outlawed astrology. The art of 'figure-casting [divination by geomancy], casting of nativities [drawing up birth charts], astrological calculations' and prophesying as a means of trying to calculate the length of life were also included in the law along with witchcraft, conjuration and sorcery. This inclusion was probably connected with the government's paranoia about seditious anti-monarchist pamphlets, often of Roman Catholic origin, speculating on how long the queen would live and predicting her date of death. Alan Macfarlane has said that the passing of the Elizabethan Witchcraft Act was because the government was worried about treasonable activity being carried out under the cloak of witchcraft and magic (1970:14).

The late Cecil Hugh Williamson, founder of the witchcraft museums on the Isle of Man and at Boscastle in Cornwall, told this writer about the so-called 'Walsingham Craft.' This he said was named after Sir Francis Walsingham, the founder of the British Secret Service in Elizabethan England. According to Williamson, it was network of witches employed by the spymaster as secret agents. Their mission was to pass on information to Walsingham about the activities of England's primary enemy the Spanish and also on any Roman Catholic plots to assassinate Queen Elizabeth. These witches were controlled by a person known as the 'Man in Black.' It has been claimed that when the Spanish Armada attempted to invade England in 1588 they were defeated not only by the brave sailors of the Royal Navy, but also by witches who by magical rituals raised the Great Storm that scattered the fleet and sunk many of their galleons.

A legal document held at the Bury St Edmunds' Record Office in Suffolk and dating from the 1580s lists the punishments to be carried out against those who broke the laws against witchcraft. It said that anyone 'presumed to be a witche, inchanter or soothsayer' was to be imprisoned until sureties were lodged on their behalf with the magistrates by relatives or friends guaranteeing their future good behavior. Interestingly, witchcraft was only classified in the document as a 'misdemeanour' along with blasphemy, fornication, drunkenness and not attending church each Sunday (Wright 2004:10).

In their religious zeal to persecute alleged witches some of the clergy in East Anglia took witchcraft laws far more seriously. In 1582 ministers were asked to report to their bishops anyone, man or woman, in their parishes who practised witchcraft, had dealings with familiar spirits, used Latin prayers and charms or consulted sorcerers and cunning folk. One Norfolk clergyman, John Parkhurst, had been exiled to continental Europe during the reign of the anti-Protestant Queen Mary I (1553–1558), who was given the grim nickname 'Bloody Mary' because three hundred Protestants were burnt at the stake during her reign. While he was in exile the Reverend Parkhurst was exposed to the anti-witch hysteria that was sweeping the Continent. When he finally returned to England in the reign of Queen Elizabeth he put into practice what he had learnt abroad about witch-hunting. As a result of his efforts at least fourteen alleged witches were indicted. Five were found guilty and hanged (ibid:13).

In 1604 Elizabeth's successor King James I (1603–1625) introduced a new Witchcraft Act that specifically dealt with the conjuration of 'wicked and evil spirits.' The king was no stranger to witchcraft because when he was James VI of Scotland he had been involved in the interrogation and prosecution of the famous North Berwick witches. In 1597 he had even written his own bestselling and influential treatise on witchcraft called *Demonologia*. As modern witch Doreen Valiente pointed out, the passing of the 1604 Witchcraft Act did not increase the number of prosecutions of people suspected of witchcraft, but it did lay the groundwork for the witch-hunt that broke out during the English Civil War and the Cromwell dictatorship that followed it (Valiente 1973:222). A witch-hunt that was instigated and led in East Anglia by the infamous witchfinder Matthew Hopkins, whose criminal and bloody career will be examined in the next chapter.

The 1604 Act proscribed excommunication and the death penalty for a wider range of offences reflecting contemporary magical practices. These included conjuring up spirits, entertaining, employing and feeding a familiar, removing corpses from graves and using their skin and bones for magical purposes, and practicing sorcery to waste, consume, destroy or kill a person. Added to the list was using magic for treasure-hunting or finding lost goods or 'to provoke a person to unlawful love.' This legislation remained in force for the next 132 years until the reign of King George II (1727–1760). It was finally replaced in 1736 and the new Witchcraft Act repealed the death penalty clause. It also stated that anyone *pretending* to practice witchcraft should be punished with a jail term. Incredibly this Georgian law was not removed from the statute books until as late as 1951.

A year after he took the throne King James I interfered in a legal case involving witchcraft in Cambridge. A man called Knightley was accused of bewitching two young women and was arrested by the city's under-sheriff. Word must have reached the ears of the king in London as the Privy Council (the ruling body of the government answerable to the monarch) sent letters about the case to the vice-chancellor of Cambridge University, the provost of King's College and the heads of Queen's College and Trinity College. The Council said the king was anxious to know if the women's illnesses had been caused by witchcraft or natural causes.

The university authorities immediately placed the two women in a safe house in the city. They then called in clergymen and doctors to examine them. Their conclusion was that, while the illness the women were suffering from was 'strange and extraordinary', it was their opinion it was quite natural. When he heard this news King James ordered Knightley to be released from custody and sent home. The king also told the university authorities to pay the women on his behalf the large sum of eighty pounds sterling to cover any hardship they had suffered (Parker 1969:160).

In East Anglia the county of Essex had the highest number of indictments for witchcraft and an overall execution rate of 27% of those convicted. Between 1560 and 1680 in England generally it is estimated that at least 2300 people were involved in cases of witchcraft either as suspects, victims or witnesses. There were over 500 known prosecutions that ended up in court, although Alan Macfarlane puts the figure slightly lower at just over 300 cases (1970:23–25). At least 30 people died in prison before their cases came to court due to the unhygienic conditions. However of 39 recorded cases that reached the courts from 1647 to 1680 it was stated that 20 were rejected and the prisoners released.

Between 1560 and 1580 when the Elizabethan Witchcraft Act was in force the offences dealt with by courts in Essex including being a sorcerer, soothsayer or diviner, finding stolen goods and identifying the thief by divination, using the 'shears and sieve' and the 'Bible and the key' to foretell the future, bewitching animals and humans, healing using magic, attending a magical ceremony where spirits or the Devil were summoned up, love magic and practicing anti-witchcraft countermagic. Some of the charges involved so-called 'black witchcraft' or the use of malefic magic to harm or kill people or livestock. At the Essex assizes in 1580, the cases involving witchcraft made up 13% of all court business. It was estimated that at this period nearly every village in the county was involved in the seeking out and prosecution of alleged witches and wizards.

Despite the number of witchcraft cases that resulted in the execution of the suspected person, L'Estrange Ewen mentions several notable instances where judges and magistrates interpreted the law in a surprisingly lenient manner. In 1592, Agnes Hales of Stebbing (Essex) escaped the gallows after being found guilty of bewitching two people to death. Instead she was sentenced to only a year in prison and several sessions in the public pillory. At the Lent Court Sessions in Essex in 1598 a male witch was sentenced to the pillory for the serious crime of 'conjuring evil spirits' that would have normally carried a heavy sentence (Ewen 1929:35–36).

One of the earliest witch trials in Cambridgeshire took place in 1466. Robert Barker of Babraham was accused of practicing witchcraft and was remanded to appear before the bishop of Ely. The trial actually took place in the Lady Chapel in the cathedral, possibly because it was consecrated ground that was believed would negate the powers of a witch, and Barker was sentenced to do penance. He had to fast every Friday (the traditional day of the Crucifixion) for twelve months and walk around the marketplaces of Ely and Cambridge on three consecutive Sundays 'carying his magickal bookes and tooles.' Afterwards these items were burnt in public and the sorcerer was forced to watch them go up in flames (Newman 1946:19).

Essex had one of its first witch trials in 1563 at Chelmsford. A woman called Elisabeth Lewys from the nearby village of Waltham was charged with the crime of 'exercysinge her wytcherie' by allegedly causing the death of several animals and humans. A prime witness at her trial, an elderly man called Henry Gaule, reported a conversation he had with the defendant's husband after accusing the couple of stealing one of his chickens. The husband had allegedly agreed that he once been 'a prettie man' when younger until his witch-wife had bewitched him and he became lame. He had found out she was responsible after consulting 'the Cunning Man of Witham' who 'pointed the finger' at her.

Another witness said she had heard a rumor that a woman called Elisabeth Lewys was a witch. When she went to her about a sore arm Lewys had told her to go see another witch at Munckewood about it. Later the witness tried to get the defendant to repay some money she was owed and Lewys refused. After this the witness' pigs sickened. One died and she had to sell off the other one. The witness' husband and child also became ill (Haining 1974: 23–26).

In July 1566 the first major witchcraft trial also took place at Chelmsford court. It was presided over by two prominent judges, Sir John Fortesque, who later became Chancellor of the Exchequer or finance minister in the government, and Sir John Southcote, who belonged to the Queen's Bench. The prosecutors of the case were a local minister, the Reverend Dr Thomas Cole, and the Attorney-General himself, Sir Gilbert Gerard. His presence suggests the government in London regarded it as an important case that would test the recently passed Witchcraft Act. Details of the trial have been recorded and preserved because they were published in a popular pamphlet called *The Examination and Confession of Certain Witches in Chelmsford in the County of Essex*.

Three defendants from the village of Hatfield Peverel a few miles from Chelmsford appeared in court charged with practicing witchcraft and consorting with familiar spirits. It was said they had terrorized the village with their magical activities. The alleged witches were Elizabeth Frauncis or Francis, Agnes Waterhouse and her daughter Joan. Frauncis was the wife of a local yeoman (somebody owning a small piece of land) and confessed she had learnt the 'arte of wytchcraft' as a young child from her now deceased grandmother Mother Eve Frauncis. She was told to denounce God and to give some of her blood on a piece of bread to a familiar spirit the old woman gave her. This took the form of a white-spotted cat called Sathan that looked like an ordinary pet except that it could speak in 'a strange hollow voice.' Elizabeth Frauncis asked the spirit to make her rich and it immediately supplied her with the means to obtain a flock of sheep.

Frauncis was accused of bewitching the new-born baby of a fellow villager William Auger so that the child became 'decrepit'. As a young woman she had also allegedly 'witched' a wealthy man called Andrew Byles who she wanted to marry. He had refused her advances and shortly afterwards had suddenly died. Frauncis was also accused of unlawfully procuring an abortion when she was pregnant with an unwanted child by using an herbal potion she had made up. When she married her present husband Frauncis does not seem to have been very happy in the relationship and caused him to become lame. She had also allegedly bewitched her own daughter who she never wanted and the child died.

The alleged witch told the court that she had kept the familiar gifted by her grandmother for fifteen or sixteen years and used it for magical purposes. After this time Frauncis gave it to her neighbor, a sixty-year old widow called Mother Agnes Waterhouse, in exchange for a home-baked cake. The new owner put the familiar into a box and it apparently turned into a toad after she recited the words 'In the Name of the Father, Sonne and Holie Ghoste' over it. Waterhouse was charged with bewitching to death another of the women's neighbor's, William Fynee, the attempted murder by witchcraft of another man, killing some hogs, curdling butter and spoiling homebrewed beer. She also confessed to saying prayers and charms in the forbidden language of Latin at a time when Protestants were persecuting Catholics. This blasphemous act was offered to the court by the prosecution as more proof she was a witch.

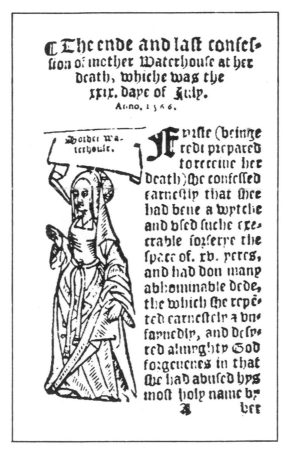

Agnes Waterhouse of Hatfield Peverel.

Mother Waterhouse's daughter, Joan, who was aged eighteen, was charged with bewitching a twelve-year-old girl, Agnes Brown, and causing her right arm and leg to become paralyzed. In her testimony before the court Brown claimed she was churning butter in the dairy when a strange creature appeared. It looked like a black dog with horns and the face of an ape and wore a silver chain and whistle around its neck. It was widely believed that a silver whistle was used by a 'master of witches' to summon the coven under his control or to conjure or call up spirits.

At the conclusion of the trial, Elizabeth Frauncis seems to have escaped fairly lightly as she was only sentenced to a year in prison. Later she appeared in a court case involving several other alleged witches and was charged with bewitching a woman called Mary Cocke. Despite it being her second offence and in theory punishable by hanging, Frauncis escaped with another year in jail and four sessions in the pillory. Her luck finally ran out in 1579. She appeared in court yet again accused of bewitching a woman called Alice Poole and was finally sent to the gallows.

Agnes Waterhouse was also condemned by the court to hang. She finally confessed her guilt on 6th July 1566 claiming that it was true she had practised sorcery for the last fifteen years. The widow said that during that period she had performed many 'abominable deeds' and asked for God's forgiveness for her crimes. On the scaffold the repentant witch yielded her soul up to Jesus Christ as her savior who 'clearly had bought her with his most precious bloudde.' Following her mother's sentencing, her daughter, Jane Waterhouse, placed herself at the mercy of the court. As a result she was found not guilty and released from custody (Hope Robins 1959:88–93 and Haining 1974: 27–37).

In 1570 Sir Thomas Smith, the son of the High Sheriff of Essex and the local Justice of the Peace near Epping Forest in Essex , and later an ambassador to the royal courts of Europe and a Secretary of State in the English government, presided over the trial of two women charged with practicing witchcraft. The first defendant, known as 'the wife of Malter', was said to have attempted to lift a bewitchment put on her husband. She had set up a trivet (iron tripod) to hold a cooking pot and placed twigs of elder and hazel wood in it. She then lit a fire under the trivet and told her husband to kneel before it and recite 'certain prayers' that were not specified in court. Unfortunately somebody witnessed this ritual and accused the woman of practicing witchcraft. In revenge Malter's wife bewitched two of the man's sheep and a sow.

One witness at the trial testified that she was a servant working for a wealthy farmer's wife in the parish of Theydon Mount. She said Goodwife Malter had called on her employer and knowing that she was going to a market in London asked her to bring back some sprats (small fish). The farmer's wife told Malter she already had enough items to bring home and refused her request. The servant woman testified that shortly afterwards the milkmaid on the farm reported that a large speckled bird of unknown type appeared in the dairy. It dipped its wings and feet in the milk pan and the liquid curdled. Attempts to ward the strange bird off with a besom (broom) failed and it also attacked the store of butter and cheese before flying away.

Another witness told Sir Thomas that another woman, Anne Vicars, charged along with Goodwife Malters, had bewitched her two years before. The victim had been stuck down with a mysterious illness causing her face to be disfigured. Her lips swelled up and turned black and as a result she was 'almost out of my wits.' Believing Vicars had hexed her, the witness consulted a cunning man called Cobham in Romford. He identified Anne Vicars as the source of her misery and told the woman that as long as he was alive the witch would have no more power over her. The victim immediately recovered and then fell sick again, although this time worse than before, when Cobham subsequently died.

Agnes Combes told the court that on the Feast of Michaelmas (September 29th) 1569 she had an argument with Anne Vicars. As a result the defendant 'fell a cunning and a banning' on her saying she would 'have her eyes.' Within two days the bewitched woman claimed she had felt ill and developed 'stabbing pains' in her eyes. Although Sir Thomas judged that there was 'much idle gossip' in the stories related by the witnesses, he committed the two women to appear before the May assizes. There they were found guilty of witchcraft and sentenced to a year in prison (Haining 1974:39–41).

Eight years after the Chelmsford case in 1574 the mother of Ellen Smyth of Maldon in Essex, where Saxons fought a famous battle with the Danes, was hanged as a known witch. It was popularly believed that her daughter had inherited her witch-mother's powers. When her father-in-law fell ill after asking Smyth for money and she refused witchcraft was suspected. He had fallen out with her over the matter and she had warned him not to do because there would be 'consequences.' Then a man that Smyth's son had asked for money was afflicted with pains all over his body when he refused to pay up. When he arrived home the victim saw a large rat run up the chimney and then a toad appeared in the room. He threw it on the fire and its body burnt with a strange unearthly blue flame. At that very moment Ellen Smyth knocked at the door (Maple 1962:49–50).

When Smyth was brought to trial she confessed to killing a young girl by witchcraft. The victim had the misfortune of quarrelling with the witch's daughter and suffered the ultimate penalty. When the girl was dying witnesses said a 'thing like a black dog' was seen standing at her bedroom door watching her. People said it was either the witch in animal form or her dark master the Devil come to claim the girl's soul (ibid). The alleged witch's son even witnessed against her in court. He confirmed the local stories that his mother had three familiar spirits she called Great Dick, Little Dick and Willet that were kept in a woolpack (a bale of wool). The court was told that Ellen Smyth's house had been searched from top to bottom when she was arrested. Several bottles had been found that were believed to be the repositories for the spirits described by her son (Macfarlane 1970:24).

In 1578 Margery Stanton of Wimbush was found guilty at the Essex quarter sessions of bewitching a gelding horse. She was also accused of tormenting a man, killing chickens and pigs, causing a woman's stomach to swell so it looked like she was pregnant, made a cow give blood instead of milk and bewitching a child so it became ill. Mother Stanton was also supposed to have used her magical powers to set an empty baby's cradle rock to and fro by just staring at it. A man who worked for the Earl of Surrey, and was therefore considered a very reliable witness, said he stabbed the cradle with his dagger because he thought the object was demonically possessed.

On another occasion Mother Stanton went begging to a neighbor's house and asked for a jug of milk. The house-owner said she had no milk to spare and told her to go away. Stanton then drew a circle on the ground with her knife outside the woman's front door. When the woman came out and asked her what she was doing Mother Stanton claimed she was just making a 'shitting hole', but she did not believe her and thought the witch was casting some kind of spell on her. This seemed to be confirmed when the woman fell ill (Macfarlane 1970:83). The circle was described in court as a 'compass' and that suggests it was of a magical nature.

People could also be taken to court for just visiting witches and cunning folk and seeking their guidance and help. In 1576 James Hopkins from Hornchurch in Essex was said to have consulted a well-known 'white witch' called Old Mother Persore. In court Hopkins said he had gone to see her in desperation because he believed his mother's cattle had been bewitched. John Shonke of Romford was also charged with consulting a cunning man called Pater (Father) Parfoot, who judging from his title may have been an ex-Catholic priest. Shonke said he would do it again even though his accusers had claimed he had rejected the true God and defied biblical law by consulting a witch (Maple 1962:39). This is a reference to a disputed phrase in the King James I Authorized Version of the Bible that states 'thou shalt not suffer a witch to live.' In the original Hebrew and Greek it has been claimed the word is actually 'poisoner.'

A mother and her daughter were indicted for practicing as witches at Cambridge in 1579. At their trial the couple freely confessed that they were witches and to 'having dealings with the Deville.' The mother told the court she had been totally loyal to her supernatural master for over thirty years. For that reason the woman refused to renounce him. She died on the gallows and it was said by onlookers that she was totally unrepentant.

The next major trial in the 16th century Essex witch-hunt was that of the St Oses or St Osyth witches, a coven of the traditional thirteen people living in a small fishing village on the coast. Again the details of the trial are well known because of the publication afterwards of a pamphlet called *A True and Just Recorde of the Information, Examination and Confession of All the Witches, taken at St Oses in the Countie of Essex* (1582). Such publications were very popular and became bestsellers. Possibly, ironically, they may have been responsible for spreading ideas about witchcraft and attracting converts to the witch-cult. It is believed that the St Osyth case and the publication of the pamphlet caused Reginald Scot, a lawyer in the county of Kent, to write his skeptical anti-witchcraft treatise *Discoverie of Witchcraft* (1584). As mentioned before, this book was used as a grimoire by witches and cunning folk because of its informative material on charms, spells and magical incantations.

It has also been claimed that the St Osyth trial may have been associated with the government's belief that there was some kind of anti-monarchist Catholic plot brewing in Essex at the time. In 1580 several suspected 'conjurors' (magicians who called up evil spirits) had been arrested in the county and sent to London to be examined by the Privy Council. Their papers and magical books had been seized and they were kept incommunicado (Rosen 1969:103) There was also talk in court circles of a conspiracy against Queen Elizabeth featuring a wax image that was to be used to 'destroy the queen's body and soul.' Three Catholic plotters, John Lee, Thomas Glascocke and Nicholas Johnson, were said to have been responsible.

The local lord of the manor and Justice of the Peace, Brian Darcye, presided over the St Osyth trial and he had already been involved in a previous case of sorcery three years earlier. A thirteen-year-old boy, Thomas Lever, had been imprisoned in the county jail at Colchester for allegedly being a sorcerer's apprentice. This had followed the arrest of William Randall from Ipswich in Suffolk for practicing conjuration in Essex to find buried treasure. In court it was said that Randall had been the leading member of a group of magicians who performed 'secret workings' near Halsted to call up 'wicked spirits' that would tell them the whereabouts of lost goods. Lever's mother contacted the Privy Council in London claiming that her son was innocent. She said he had not been Randall's magical assistant and therefore should not be locked up in prison. The Council wrote to Lord Darcye and said they knew no good reason why the child had been imprisoned. Under the circumstances he should therefore be released.

In the St Osyth trial Lord Darcye, who became the county sheriff three years later and was conversant with the writings of the French witch-hunter Jean Bodin, took the unusual step of interrogating each of the defendants. The trial took place in Chelmsford in February 1582. A witness called Grace Thurlowe told Lord Darcye that one of the defendants, Ursel or Ursula Kempe or Gray, had visited her house when her son Davy was ill and kept asking about his health. This concern was enough to make her suspicious and she interpreted the query as some kind of charm by Kempe. It seemed to have worked as after a visit by Kempe the child slept well and eventually he recovered. Thurlowe then gave birth to another child but when Kempe volunteered to be its nurse she refused her offer. Shortly afterwards the child fell out of its cradle and broke its neck and Thurlow suspected that Kempe was a witch and may have been responsible.

Despite this when Kempe offered to heal Thurlowe, who was suffering from 'a lameness in the bones', probably arthritis, she agreed. The cure that Kempe used was one she had gotten from a cunning woman she herself had consulted when also suffering from 'the lameness.' It consisted of taking a lump of hog dung and mixing it with a bunch of the herb chervil. This was then held in the left hand while the mixture was pricked three times with a knife held in the right hand. The dung and the herbs were then thrown on a fire. The knife was then used to make 'three prickes' under the kitchen table and left sticking in the wood until the lameness went away. Three sage leaves and some flowers of St John Wort were to be placed in a large mug of ale. The patient had to drink some of the liquid first thing in the morning and last thing at night until it all gone and then they would be cured.

After Grace Thurlowe recovered from her ailment, Ursula Kempe asked her for a payment of twelve pennies. Thurlowe said she was 'a poor and needy woman' and could not afford to pay the fee. In response Kempe said in that case she could give her a piece of cheese instead. When Thurlowe did not have any cheese to give her either, Kempe said she would get even with her. The lameness in her legs then came back and in fact became so bad that Thurlowe could not get out of bed unaided (Davies 2003:12).

A young child called John or Thomas Rabbett, who it seems was one of Ursula Kempe's illegitimate children, was called to give evidence against his mother in court. He said that he knew she owned four familiar spirits; a gray cat called Tittey, a white lamb called Tyffin, a black toad called Pignine, and a black cat called Jacke. The boy claimed that he had often seen his mother feeding these spirits with beer, bread and her own blood. She sent forth these creatures to punish, injure and kill those who had crossed her. Other child witnesses were called to give evidence against the other defendants. They said their parents and grandparents also possessed familiar spirits that took the shape of a goose, a blackbird, a rat, a cow, a black dog and even fantastically a tiny horse and a lion.

Ursula Kempe herself was called to give evidence and Lord Dayce promised that if she told the truth he would deal with her favorably. Kempe accepted the offer in good faith and made a full confession. She said that it was true that she had sent her familiars to destroy cattle and also to throw Grace Thurlowe's baby out of its cot. She further confessed to using witchcraft to kill her brother's wife because she had maliciously called Kempe a 'whore and witch'. Believing that she would be set free because of this confession, Kempe then named several other people who she knew were also witches. In fact at the end of the trial

Kempe and another female defendant were found guilty and hanged. The rest of the accused were also found guilty, but their deaths sentences were repealed or they were acquitted (Rosen 1969, Haining 1974 and Maple 1962).

A skeleton said to have been that of Ursula Kempe was exhibited for many years in Cecil Williamson's Museum of Witchcraft at Boscastle in Cornwall. Allegedly after the execution of the two St Osyth witches they were refused a Christian burial and were instead interred in unconsecrated ground. Four centuries later, in 1921, a builder called Charlie Brooker bought a row of old cottages in Mill Street, St Osyth and planned to renovate them. He rented a house in nearby Colchester Street while the work went on. One day he was digging for sand to use in the building work and uncovered some human remains. Archaeologists established that the bones were several hundred years old and belonged to two skeletons. They had been buried on a pre-Christian (pagan) north-south axis instead of facing east and large iron rivets had been driven through the bones of the wrists, knees and ankles. This was an old custom used to bind the earthbound spirits of witches and suicides and stop them 'night walking' or haunting the living.

Brooker decided to make some money by exhibiting the better preserved of the skeletons (believed to have been Ursula Kempe's) to the public. He charged people sixpence each to view the remains that were exhibited in a specially made wooden box like a coffin. He also printed and distributed a leaflet about the exhibition and curious folk came from miles around to gawp at the bones. In 1933 the Brookers were living in one of the now renovated cottages when a fire broke out and they narrowly escaped with their lives. Superstitious gossip blamed the inferno on the 'witch's curse' and the skeleton was hastily reburied under the kitchen floor of the cottage.

There it remained until 1957 when Charlie Brooker's son-in-law dug it up and tried to revive the exhibition of the skeleton to the paying public. No good came from this new enterprise and local protests forced him to abandon it. Instead in 1964 he decided to sell the skeleton of Ursula Kempe to Cecil Williamson. He placed it in a specially made elm coffin lined with purple satin and exhibited it at first at his Cornish witchcraft museum and then at his House of Shells museum at Buckfastleigh, Devon. After he retired in 1999 and sold his museums, Williamson arranged for the skeleton to be placed in the safe hands of a friend of his, a well-known controversial and eccentric artist in

Plymouth. It is not known what happened to the skeleton after the artist himself died a few years later (Harris 2001).

Several of the victims in the St Osyth trial consulted cunning folk to try and counteract the bewitchments they believed they were under. Thomas D'eath said he visited a physician for advice because he believed his daughter had been put under a spell by the witches. He took a sample of her urine for the doctor to examine and asked him if witchcraft was the cause of her health problems. The physician refused to give a straight answer to the man's question. D'eath then decided to consult a cunning man (Davies 2003:78). Robert Sannever told the court that he had employed the daughter of one of the accused, Elizabeth Eustance, as a servant. One day he chastised the girl because of her 'lewd speeches' and rude behavior. The next day Sannever was sitting by the fire when his face was sudden 'twisted strangely'—symptoms resembling those of a stroke. He said he was cured of this complaint by 'one of skill' (i.e., a cunning person), who also advised him to dismiss the servant girl from his employment as she had been responsible for his affliction. No action was taken against these two witnesses for admitting they had consulted cunning people.

Following this incident, the feud between Sannever and Mother Eustance continued for many years. When his brother-in-law claimed the woman had bewitched him, Sannever threatened the witch with having a red-hot poker being placed across her bare buttocks. In response to this threat of physical violence, Mother Eustance said that while Sannever's pregnant wife was fit and well now she would soon be otherwise. In fact his wife died from complications shortly after giving birth to their expected child (Briggs 1997:151).

A third witch trial took place in Chelmsford in 1589 with again a pamphlet being published and sold afterwards to mark the event. As in the previous cases, the judges selected to try the alleged witches were important Establishment figures—an aristocrat called Baron Robert Clarke and the Queen's Serjeant, John Rikering. This is a further indication that the authorities were taking accusations of witchcraft seriously. Again children were brought before the court to give evidence against the accused who were their mothers and grandmothers. When the guilty verdicts were returned in a travesty of justice the child witnesses were congratulated for telling the truth about their families and helping to secure the convictions of their family members.

Four of those accused came from the Dagenham, Essex area and they were Joan Cunny or Coney, her daughter Alice, Joan Upney and Joan Prentice. Cunny was said to have been instructed in the art of witchcraft by a woman known as Mother Humphrey of Maplestead. She was told to draw a circle on the ground, kneel inside it and call upon the 'chief of the devils.' Cunny said she had performed the ritual twenty years before in a field belonging to a gentleman called John Wiseman (sic) of Stisted. The suggestion was that he was somehow involved in the witchery. Two spirits in the shape of large black frogs appeared and promised to provide her with anything Cunny wanted for the rest of her life. The only catch was that in return they wanted her soul. She agreed and gave the spirits the names 'Jack and Jill.' The witch took them home and kept them in a wooden box, feeding them daily on bread and milk.

Joan Upney also confessed to having a familiar that took the shape of a mole. It was given to her six or seven years earlier by another witch from Barking called Fustian Kirtle Whitecoat. When the mole died twelve months later Whitecoat gave her two more familiars, a mole and a toad, to replace her loss. She later acquired some more toads and Upney added that although her eldest daughter would have nothing to do with the familiars, her younger daughter was not afraid of them. In fact she used them for magical purposes unspecified in court.

The third of the accused women, Joan Prentice, was living in an almshouse at Sible Hadingham when she was arrested. This establishment had been founded by a charity for the provision of the poor. When the case came to court Prentice confessed that 'between the Feast of All Saints [November 1st] and the birth of Our Lord God [Christmas Day]' the Devil appeared to her. It was, she said, about ten of the clock at night and Old Nick took the form of a large brown colored ferret with large 'fiery eyes' that spoke to her in a gruff voice.

The animal stood on a wooden stool on its hind legs, placed its forepaws in her lap and stared into her eyes. To her amazement the ferret then spoke to her and demanded she give it her immortal soul. She was so astonished to hear the animal speaking that she cried out; 'In the Name of God, who art thou?' and the ferret replied it had nothing to do with God and was the Devil. Prentice said that her soul belonged to Jesus Christ, but this did not stop the demonic creature demanding a few drops of her blood to drink from the forefinger of her left hand. This vampiric act apparently placed the woman under its power. Similar visitations continued for some time until Prentice sent the ferret out to bite the child of one of her neighbors who had annoyed her. When it returned from its mission the spirit said that he had bitten the child as she had asked and as a result it had died. Prentice told the court she bravely chastised the ferret for disobeying her orders and called him 'a villain.' The spirit was obviously annoyed at this as it vanished and she never saw it again.

Joan Prentis. Jack and Jill, and other familiars, are also pictured.

All four women were found guilty of practicing witchcraft, although Alice Cunny seems to have escaped the death penalty because she was pregnant. As a result her life and that of her unborn child were spared by the judges. The other three women were all hanged in indecent haste less than two hours after the sentence as passed. A minister, Master Ward, was present at the execution at the request of the judges and he extorted the women to repent their sins. He said they should show the large crowd, who had gathered to see the execution on a specially constructed triple gallows, the truth of their wickedness and to call on God for his mercy and pardon. The women reluctantly repeated a few prayers said by Ward and prompted by the minister said they deserved to die for their 'wicked sins' and therefore accepted their fate. Mother Upney admitted that she had 'grievously sinned' by giving her soul to the Devil and he had deceived her. It was said by witnesses to the executions that Upney died as a penitent. The alleged witch asked for 'God and the world' to forgive her because she had led such a 'wicked and detestable life' (Rosen 1969: 182–189).

On a cold November's day in 1589 one of the five daughters of Robert and Elizabeth Throckmorton living in the Huntingdonshire village of Warboys fell ill with a mysterious illness. She began suffering from persistent bouts of violent sneezing leading to nose bleeds and her arms and legs shook uncontrollably. The manor house where she lived was next to the parish church and the ringing of its bells calling the faithful to prayer appeared to trigger these strange fits. Four years later in 1593 the Throckmorton's neighbors, Alice and John Samuels, were brought to court charged with sorcery.

On November 12th 1589 an elderly woman, Alice Samuels, had visited the Throckmortons, a wealthy family who had just moved into the village. For several days their nine-year-old daughter Jane had been sick and having heard about it Samuels called at the house to enquire after her. Unfortunately while she was in the house the girl got worse and cried out; 'Look where the old witch sits. Did you ever see one more like a witch then she is? Take off her knitted black cap, for I cannot abide to look at her.' When Samuels left Jane experienced a temporary relapse from her symptoms, although the fits soon began again.

At this stage the family were still seeking a rational reason for their daughter's sickness and Mrs Throckmorton was at first annoyed her daughter had accused the old woman of being a witch. They sent a sample of her urine to a doctor in Cambridge and he diagnosed the patient was suffering from a bad attack of intestinal worms. He prescribed a herbal remedy made from wormwood and horehound mixed with milk, honey and liquorice syrup to drive the parasites from her body. Unfortunately this did not work and the fits continued.

When a further sample of urine was sent to the same doctor he then concluded that there was nothing physically ailing the girl. He suggested that possibly her illness was a case of bewitchment and a supernatural agency was involved. The parents at first rejected the doctor's theory and sought a second opinion from a prominent physician at Clare College, Cambridge. He also diagnosed worms as the cause of the daughter's health problems and recommended the same remedy as his medical colleague.

When in early 1590 two of the Throckmorton's other daughters also fell ill and in their agony cried out the name of Alice Samuels the family began to suspect witchcraft might actually be involved. The alleged appearance of Samuel's fetch or spirit double in the girls' bedroom during the night seemed to confirm this theory, even though the family could not understand why the apparently harmless old lady should work malefic magic against the family. The daughters had reported that they woke up in the night and saw the old woman standing at the bottom of the bed with a evil look on her face.

In the meantime Mother Samuels had wisely decided to keep away from the manor house and had stopped her well-meaning visits. The local gossips however believed she was responsible for the ill-health of the Throckmorton daughters. Then the youngest daughter, Grace, and her elder sister Joan, both of whom had been healthy up to then also fell ill with the same symptoms as the other daughters. Joan also denounced Alice Samuels as a witch after telling her parents she had seen a vision of the old woman in the house.

Events began to accelerate out of control in February 1590 when Gilbert Pickering, the brother of Elizabeth Throckmorton, visited the house from his home in Northamptonshire. He fancied himself as an amateur witchfinder and decided to take matters into his hands by visiting and interrogating Alice Samuels. He forced her to return with him to the manor house together with her daughter and two women that local gossips had also branded as 'witches'. As soon as the children saw Samuels and the other women they fell on the floor writhing around like 'grounded fish taken out of the water.' At this hysterical outburst Pickering became convinced that the girls were possessed by evil spirits sent by Samuels and her daughter.

In 1592, after a series of events, often violent, during which Gilbert Pickering and the Throckmortons tried to force Alice Samuels to confess of her own accord to bewitching the girls, Robert Throckmorton visited her cottage. He tried to force her and her daughter to accompany him to see the bishop of Lincoln. When they refused to co-operate he sent for the parish constable and told him to arrest both women. When this did not happen Robert Throckmorton then tricked Samuels into confessing that she was a witch and her confession was overheard by villagers hiding outside the window of the room.

On St Stephen's Day (December 26th) 1592 Mother Samuels and her daughter Agnes were finally brought before a church court presided over by the bishop of Lincoln. Alice Samuels was questioned at great length and confessed she had suckled a familiar spirit in the shape of a hen and fed it with her blood. Samuels said she harmed the Throckmorton children using witchcraft and had been taught how to by an 'upright man,' a term for a wandering peddler and also a popular nickname for the Devil. Both women were committed to a secular court and sent to Huntingdon prison to await trial at the next sessions in January 1593. Meanwhile Alice Samuels husband, John, had also been accused of being a 'a wikked man and a wytch' and of bewitching to death an aristocrat called Lady Cowell.

On April 5th 1593 Alice, Agnes and John Samuel appeared in court charged under the Witchcraft Act of practicing 'conjurations, enchantments and bewitchments'. At the trial Robert Throckmorton accused the Samuels of bewitching his wife and daughters and also of 'speaking rudely' to his calves and pigs so they became sick. The chief jailer at Huntingdon prison also gave evidence that when Samuels was there his manservant had chained her to a bedpost in her cell as a punishment. Shortly afterwards the man became unwell and suffered violent fits until he died five or six days later.

The presiding judge found the Samuels guilty as charged and sentenced them to be executed. The next day they were visited in jail by several clergymen who advised them to repent and confess all their sins. At first Mother Samuels refused until on her walk to the gallows she broke down and confessed again to bewitching the Throckmorton family. When the cleric asked her to recite the Lord's Prayer she stumbled over the words and then told him she did not believe in God or the Church's teachings. This was an ultimate blasphemy at the time. After the execution, in a final act of indignity, Alice Samuel's corpse was stripped naked and examined for evidence of the 'witches' mark.' In a 'secret place' (vagina) a small lump of flesh about an inch long was found—perhaps her clitoris. This discovery was offered as sure proof that the executed woman had been guilty and justice had truly been done.

In 2008 the governors of a primary school in Warboys that had received poor inspection reports and had difficulty in recruiting teachers decided that the school's logo of a witch on a broomstick was giving it a negative public image. Unfortunately the pupils at the school disagreed and they started a campaign to prevent the witchy image, obviously connected to the Alice Samuels case, being removed from its letterheads. They were supported in this campaign by many local people ('Spare the Witches of Warboys' *Daily Mail*, 18th April 2008).

At Kings Lynn, Norfolk in 1590 Margaret Read was one of the very few women in England to be actually burnt at the stake as a witch. This was because she had been found guilty of the specialist crime of 'petty treason' for bewitching her husband to death. According to folklorist Nigel Pennick, the wall of a house in the marketplace at Kings Lynn has a diamond-shaped decoration with a stylized heart in its center. This is supposed to mark the place where Margaret Read's blood splattered when her heart exploded from her body in the extreme heat of the pyre. Two other East Anglian women were also burned at the stake for witchcraft; Mother Lakeland at Ipswich in 1654 and Mary Oliver in Norwich five years later. Again both had been accused of bewitching their husbands to death (Pennick 1995:31).

Mother Lakeland's defense in court was that she had been a 'professor of religion' for many years. Apparently this was somebody who had studied the subject in some depth. Yet by her own admission she had been a witch for over twenty years after signing a pact giving her soul to the Devil. In return the Horned One had promised her anything she wanted during her life if she served him well. He then presented her with three familiars in the shape of two small dogs and a mole. Lakeland used these spirits to bewitch people she hated, including her unwanted husband who as a result of her witchcraft became ill and died.

In the same year two Quakers found themselves before the magistrates charged with bewitching Margaret Prior of Longstanton. Their trial was recorded in three pamphlets, one written by Cambridge University scholars, one by John Bunyan, author of the famous *A Pilgrim's Progress,* and the third by a group of Quakers attacking the other two publications. When the case came to court the charges against one of the Quakers were dropped after a personal request from their alleged victim Margaret Prior. However she bizarrely told the court that another of the defendants, Widow Morlin, had transformed her into a mare by a magical spell and ridden her to Madingly Hall. She was left tied outside while the defendant went inside and feasted on rabbit and mutton with its aristocratic owner.

Not surprisingly perhaps, the presiding judge, Justice Windham, was not convinced by this fantastic tale. He closely questioned Margaret Prior in the witness box and demanded to know why it had taken her so long to make her accusations. He also queried her claim to have been changed into a horse by witchcraft. Finally the judge dismissed Prior's claims as 'a dream and a phantasie.' He ordered that the accused widow should be released without a blemish on her character.

Jane Margaret Wyseman of Malden was accused by Thomas Wardell in 1591 of practicing witchcraft. Wyseman turned on her accuser and vehemently denied any wrongdoing. Because Wardell was unable to provide any firm evidence to support his claim she was released from custody. However her accuser was not so lucky. The magistrates ordered that he should be bound over to keep the peace in the future and make no more false accusations against alleged witches.

This however was not the end of the matter as shortly afterwards Jane Wyseman was accused again by someone else of being a witch. In a strange turnaround her former accuser Thomas Wardell appeared in court on her behalf as a character witness. He told the magistrates that previously he had never 'reported that he saw [the] broome sweepe the house, alone, without [her] handes, nor had he any case to say [so].' Many people in the court wondered exactly what Wardell was referring to in his evidence, but his testimony for the defense was enough to help Wyseman get acquitted again (Morgan 1973:59–60).

Aristocrats, as in other parts of the British Isles, were not safe from accusations of witchcraft. When the divorce case relating to the failed marriage of Robert Deveraux, the Earl of Essex, came before the courts in 1613 his wife said he practised witchcraft. She told the court that as a result of his 'diabolical practices' her husband had become impotent. As he a result he had been unable to consummate their marriage. For that reason she asked the judge to grant her an annulment so she could remarry and based on the evidence provided it was duly given.

In 1653 Giles Fenderley's executed body was hanged in chains in the gibbet on Leaven Heath near Nayland in Suffolk. He had confessed to making a pact with the Devil and of murdering his own wife. Fenderley had served as a soldier in the English army in Flanders and boasted he had survived being hit by several musket balls because of his satanic covenant. In his defense, such as it was, he claimed that the Devil had accepted his wife's life in exchange for the magical powers he had granted him. Fendeley claimed he had no choice but to kill her as a sacrifice so he could keep his bargain with the Horned One (Wright 2004:34).

At the busy port of Lowestoft in Suffolk in 1664 Amy Dury and Rose Cullender were found guilty of bewitching young women. Samuel Pacy alleged that his two daughters had suffered from violent fits after the defendants had come to his house selling fresh fish from boats in the harbor. The children claimed that Dury and Cullender had then appeared later in their bedrooms and also sent their familiars to torment them. As a result of this psychic attack the girls had lost the use of their limbs, were struck dumb and were allegedly seen to vomit up pins, needles and nails. Once they caught a mouse and when they, rather cruelly, threw it in the fire it exploded 'like gunpowder' so they knew it was one of the witches' familiars.

At the trial the girls experienced more fits and fainted when they saw the two women. One cried out in fear: 'Burn her! Burn her!' Dury and Cullender denied all the charges and swore they were innocent of causing the girls' condition. A doctor called to give evidence in their defense said that in his opinion the girls were suffering from hysteria. However when questioned he backtracked and admitted that their condition could have been caused by diabolical forces working through the alleged witches. Another of the witnesses said he believed the girls were just play-acting to get attention. Despite this skeptical testimony the judge found Dury and Cullender guilty and sentenced them to death by hanging.

In 1672 at the village of Saxmundham (an old name dating from the Anglo-Saxon period) in Suffolk an eighteen year-old maid at the local vicarage suddenly became ill. She told her concerned employer it felt like somebody was pricking her in the leg with a needle. As the illness progressed she allegedly began to vomit up small bodkins, pieces of bone and eggshell and a row of pins stuck in a piece of blue paper. The doctor called in to examine the maid said he could find nothing physically wrong with her. It was therefore suspected that witchcraft was involved. The burden of guilt was placed on an old woman the servant girl had quarreled with over the possession of a bright new pin. The maid eventually recovered and there is no indication that the alleged bewitcher was ever charged.

Seven years later at Whissonsett in Norfolk four women, Elizabeth Blade, Mary English, Lizzie Crowe and Ursula Skippon, were arrested after allegations they were witches and imprisoned in Norwich Castle.

English confessed to setting fire to two houses and sending her familiar in the shape of a white mouse to a fellow witch, Goodwife Dunham, who died five days later. She also accused another defendant Lizzie Crowe of being a witch. As proof she told the court Crowe had several extra nipples on her arm and the side of body. According to English, Crowe had sent her own familiar spirit in the shape of a duck to kill a man called John Willis.

Several witnesses came forward to confirm in court that the accused women were well known witches. One witness said that each of the women was as bad as the other. In fact if they were not imprisoned soon they would 'bring the whole town to ruin.' It would appear that there was some kind of local vendetta against the women by other women. The judge was not convinced by the testimony of either English or the witnesses and he told all the defendants they were free to leave the court and go home.

As the 17th century drew to a close judges and magistrates were beginning to become more skeptical about allegation concerning witchcraft. In the spring of 1694 Justice Holt presided over the Suffolk Lent Sessions. He heard several indictments against Phillipa Munnings for being a witch. It was said she had threatened her landlord, Thomas Pannell, when they had a dispute by telling him: 'Thy nose shalt lie upwards in the churchyard before Sunday next.'

A witness was brought before the judge and testified that Munnings had two imps or familiars, one colored white and one black, which she kept in a wicker basket. Another witness said the witch had a third familiar in the shape of a wild polecat. Justice Holt refused to accept the 'evidence' provided and dismissed the case (Wright 2004:370). When Judge Holt died a monument was erected in his honor. The inscription on it praised the judge as 'The watchful upholder, the keen defender, the brave guardian of liberty and the law of England.' He was one of several magistrates and judges who were beginning to question the validity of cases involving alleged witches.

If the legal profession was becoming more skeptical concerning witchcraft the clergy in East Anglia were still trying their best to keep the subject alive. In 1699 the Reverend James Boys of Coggleshall investigated the case of a local widow who had been talking to anyone who would listen about her intimate relationship with Devil. The vicar called on the woman to question her about the claims. As a test he asked her to join him in reciting the Lord's Prayer and she was unable to remember the words or complete it. Then, amazingly, with the clergy-man's approval, a mob 'swam' the widow in a local pond to ascertain if she was a witch or not. As a result of this harsh punishment the woman became ill and died a few weeks later. After her death the abuse of the poor woman continued as Boys ordered the undertakers to strip her body naked to look for the so-called 'witch's mark' (Davies 1999:85).

3

The Witchfinder-General

EAST ANGLIA WAS the first region in England to support Parliament against King Charles I (reigned 1625–1649) in the dispute over his divine right to rule. The period of the English Civil War between the royalists and the Parliamentarians, led by General Oliver Cromwell, a Cambridgeshire landowner and farmer, saw an increase in witch-hunting. Not only were there more trials in the ten years from 1640 to 1650, but a new phenomenon of professional witch-hunters arose. An additional legal dimension to the situation was added by the temporary suspension of the court system and the breakdown of central government during the war when the king moved his court from London to Oxford. The legal system in areas that supported the Parliamentary party was replaced by one based on local religious groups, predominantly Puritan in nature, localized law enforcement by lords of the manor and vigilante actions.

For instance in 1645 in Essex, where many of the witch trials took place during the war, the assizes were not presided over by a circuit judge from London as was normally the case. Instead a special court was convened under the control and direction of the Earl of Warwick. He had not received any training in the law or legal matters and was just an aristocrat representing the local military authority and supporting the Parliamentary cause. This was repeated all over East Anglia as political authority shifted slowly after each lost battle from the royalist government based in Oxford to those areas that championed the dictator Cromwell and his rebel New Model Army.

The mass anxiety, social disruption and unrest caused by the civil war created superstitious fears in the stressed-out population. As in any wartime situation, including the First World War in the 20th century, there was a sudden demand for talismans and charms by both sides irrespective of their religious beliefs. In turn this played into the hands of the many witches and cunning folk who supplied them. Eric Maple has said that the wise women 'did a roaring trade in protective amulets, including effigies of imps, which they sold to soldiers. In a magical age the prospect of death must have tempted many to return to their ancient faith in magic, overcoming their Puritan scruples' (1962:80–81).

These superstitious and magical beliefs permeated all levels of society, both royalist and Puritan, Cavalier and Roundhead. King Charles I was said to consult astrologers for advice on warfare tactics and as will be seen the royalist soldier Prince Rupert was supposed to have a familiar spirit in the form of a small dog. Even the future Lord Protector of England, Oliver Cromwell, was not unfamiliar with witchcraft. In 1593 when his grandmother died, a couple and their daughter were charged at Huntingdon assizes with bewitching her to death. They were hanged and all their goods were granted to Cromwell's grandfather, who was the local lord of the manor, as compensation for his wife's fate. He refused to take the goods and ordered them to be auctioned off instead. The proceeds were used to fund a daily sermon preached against the sin of witchcraft by a minister at Queen's College, Cambridge (Stirling Taylor 1978).

Cromwell was popularly believed to have sold his soul to the Devil for victory in his battles against the royalist forces. Before the Battle of Dunbar it was said a mysterious 'man in black' had appeared in the Parliamentary camp and was seen going into the general's tent and he never came out. Allegedly Cromwell and the stranger, who was the Devil, had haggled over the price of the soldier's soul. When Cromwell died there was a terrifying thunderstorm and dogs barked all night before his passing. The superstitious said that was a sign that the Old One had come during the night when the Lord Protector was dying and claimed his soul as agreed in their bargain.

It was in this fevered and stressful atmosphere of religious intolerance, superstition and a blind belief in demonic forces that witch-hunting flourished. The period 1645–1667 has been described as 'the most remarkable episode in the history of English, and indeed European, witchcraft' (Sharpe 1996:128). In that relatively short period nineteen alleged witches were executed in Essex alone. Over a hundred suspects were 'examined' in Suffolk and of those forty were sent to trial. Many of those who were found guilty were hanged. Another forty people appeared before the courts or tribunals in Norfolk and half of those were executed. In Huntingdonshire eight people were prosecuted for practicing witchcraft and five of those were sentenced to death and this was the tip of the iceberg in East Anglia.

Many of these witch trials and executions were the responsibility of one man who waged a brief but bloody two-year campaign of terror across the countryside—the so-called 'Witchfinder-General' Matthew Hopkins. Dr Malcolm Gaskill of Churchill College, Cambridge has described him as 'physically slight' with a personality that was 'hot-headed, impetuous, edgy, devious, charismatic and persuasive' (*Secret History: The Witchfinders*, Channel 4 television documentary). James Sharpe described him as 'an obscure petty gentleman' (1996:128), while Tom Gardner says he was 'a terrible liar' (1981:44).

A contemporary engraving of the Witchfinder-General depicts a short, slightly built and serious faced young man. He has fair shoulder-length hair and a neat moustache and goatee beard in the Cavalier style. Hopkins was always well dressed in fashionable black clothes and in the engraving he wears a Swiss-type buttoned cloak and a matching tunic or waistcoat. His trousers are tucked into knee-length riding boots complete with spurs. He holds a staff and was always accompanied everywhere by his favorite pet greyhound.

Matthew Hopkins was a character whose origins are obscure because little was heard of him before 1643–44, although his career as a witch-hunter for the next few years was well documented in court records and popular pamphlets about the trials he was involved in. When Hopkins died in 1647 the entry for his burial in the parish register of Mildey-cum-Manningtree in Essex said he was the son of a John Hopkins, the wealthy minister of Great Wenham near Colchester. He was described as a Church of England (Anglican) clergyman and 'preacher of the Word of God'. His biographer Richard Deacon has suggested that Matthew Hopkins was born around 1619 and therefore would have been around thirty years old when he died.

Hopkins himself told his friend the astrologer William Lilly (an odd friendship under the circumstances) that he came from a long line of Suffolk schoolmasters. He also boasted to the royalist aristocrat Lady Jane Whorwood when he was trying to befriend her that he was the grandson of an English Catholic diplomat who worked in the Low Countries (modern Holland, Belgium and Luxembourg). In fact the Hopkins family did have ancestral links with Holland as his relatives included Dutch and French Huguenots (Protestants).

Hopkins appeared to have been well-educated as he could both read and write Latin. After leaving school he had studied maritime law in Amsterdam and worked for a Dutch company selling shipping insurance. Richard Deacon suspected that this may have been when he met William Lilly as the astrologer was employed by maritime insurers to use his occult art to assess the risks of ships sinking. He also investigated missing vessels and those lost at sea in incidents believed to be the work of storm-raising witches (1976:20).

As a child Matthew Hopkins had been brought up in the Essex town of Manningtree and would have heard stories about witchcraft. One incident in particular that occurred in his youth seems to have influenced his later decision to hunt down suspected witches. This was a case at Dedham in Essex when 'evil spirits' had appeared to a Mr Earl in the form of two people he knew. Possibly he had seen their 'fetches', astral or spirit-doubles known as 'living phantoms.' Hopkins always remembered this story and it strengthened his belief in the reality of the supernatural and witchcraft.

Hopkins had also studied the local history of witchcraft. One of his first witch-finding expeditions was carried out in the Essex village of Leighs. Hopkins had visited it to see if any traces of witchcraft had survived there from the time of the 16th century dissolution of the monasteries in the reign of King Henry VIII. The last prior of Leighs Priory had been removed from his position on the orders of the king. He was given the living in the village of Blackmore and was later prosecuted for practicing the 'Black Art' and alchemy.

Although he was not the first professional witchfinder, Matthew Hopkins was the only to adopt the invented title of the 'Witchfinder-General.' This reflected the fact that his activities eventually extended beyond his native Essex to include Suffolk, Norfolk, Cambridgeshire, Huntingdonshire, the Isle of Ely and even as far afield as Bedfordshire and Northamptonshire. However in 1643 and 1644 he was still working as a lawyer in Manningtree and Ipswich in Suffolk. In that period he carried out a personal investigation of witchcraft in the Essex marshes popularly believed to be the haunt of witches, ghosts and smugglers. It

Matthew Hopkins, Witchfinder General.

was an area well known for its strange mix of superstitious beliefs, anti-Catholicism, anti-royalist Puritanism and extreme religious intolerance.

As well as researching local accounts about alleged witchcraft Hopkins also read widely on the subject. His bedtime reading included King James I's *Daemonologie* (1597), Thomas Potts' account of the trial in 1612 of the famous Pendle witches in Lancashire, who may have been crypto-Catholics, William Perkins' *A Discourse of the Damned Arte of Witchcraft* (1608) and Richard Berhard's influential *Guide Book to Grand Jury-Men*. It has also been suggested that during Hopkins' time in Holland he may have been exposed to the ideas and methods used by Continental witch-hunters. He certainly believed that the members of the English witch-cult practised 'devil worship' as witches in European countries accused of being heretics were supposed to.

This extensive study and research may also have been added to by Hopkins' belief that he himself was the victim of malefic witchcraft. One reason why he launched his witch-hunting crusade was that he believed a coven were meeting secretly near his house in Manningtree and performing magical rituals to bring about his death. He claimed that the witches met every six weeks on a Friday night with others attending from nearby towns. At these gatherings, which sound suspiciously like Witches' Sabbaths, he said the witches offered 'solemne sacrifices' to their dark master the Devil. Hopkins also told people that a 'black thing, like a catte, but thrice as bigge' came into his yard in the middle of the night. It sat on a strawberry bed and then jumped the pale (fence) when Hopkins' greyhound chased it away. The poor dog came back trembling with fear. He is also supposed to have seen a horrible apparition of the Devil that manifested in his bed chamber during the night.

Robin Briggs has said that Matthew Hopkins' reign of terror 'was only possible at a time when central authority had broken down.' In fact Briggs claims that if the royalist government had still been in charge in East Anglia then Hopkins' witch-hunt would have either not started or would have been stopped at a very early stage (1997:192). In fact in the period from 1644 to 1645 when Hopkins first began his witch-hunting activities the royalist forces were losing battles at the hands of the Roundheads and faced defeat.

The Witchfinder-General was accompanied in his activities across the countryside in East Anglia by a deputy assistant called John Stearne and three principal female assistants, Mary Phillips, Priscilla Briggs and Frances Mills. This company helped him to seek out, interrogate and process his victims. The women were paid twelve pence a day for their services and were experienced midwives. They examined the naked and shaved bodies of suspected witches for evidence of the so-called *Diablo stigmata* or 'Devil's Mark' given to them at their initiation and for the extra teats or nipples they used to suckle their familiar spirits.

Hopkins also employed local people from the hamlets, villages and towns he visited. These hired hands included 'ancient and skillful matrons and midwives' who were involved in 'pricking' suspects to find the Mark. This was done with either a long pin or a special metal bodkin with a handle and a long sharp pointed end. Suspects were stripped naked, all their body hair was shaved off and they were blindfolded. The pricker then probed various parts of the body, especially the genitalia, with the sharp end of the bodkin. This was because it was believed the place where the Devil had marked a witch was insensitive to pain and they would not feel the instrument. Sometimes the witchfinders employed a false bodkin whose pointed ends retracted into a hollow handle or shaft so they were guaranteed to always find the witches' mark (Robbins 1959:399).

The company of witchfinders that accompanied Hopkins on his travels were given various titles describing their role. Discoverers were those who researched and hunted out witches. Matrons were prickers, Watchers observed suspects in prison to see if they were visited by their familiars, and to make sure they did not fall asleep, Walkers, as the name suggested, 'walked' prisoners up and down until they were exhausted and confessed, and finally Swimmers were responsible for the 'swimming' of suspected witches in ponds and rivers to find out if they were guilty. Although torture was not allowed, sleep deprivation, starving and beating suspects took place and was ignored by the authorities. Confessions obtained from such practices was often accepted as evidence of guilt in court cases.

Hopkins also employed a wide network of informers who supplied him with intelligence, usually based on rumor and gossip, about alleged witchcraft activities and people suspected of being witches and cunning folk or of consulting them. One of these informers was a clergyman, the Reverend Joseph Long, the minister at Great Clacton (Essex). This system of informing often led to baseless and false accusations being made against perceived enemies or rivals and the prosecution of the innocent.

There is some evidence that some of those accused were mentally ill or suffering from senile dementia. One classic example was a man who traveled twelve miles, which was a long way in those days, to confess to Hopkins that he was a witch and that he deserved to be punished. Despite the fact that he was obviously mentally disturbed, the so-called witch was duly arrested by the authorities on the witchfinder's recommendation. He was tried, found guilty and hanged for the non-existent crimes he had confessed to in his madness.

Hopkins and his gang often invited themselves to the towns they visited by first writing in advance to the town councilors or magistrates offering their services to find witches. In one of his early cases in 1645 Hopkins wrote to the magistrate of one Essex town saying one of its inhabitants had invited him to visit the place. The purpose of his visit was to search for 'evil disposed persons, called witches.' He also said that word had reached him that the local minister is 'farre agin us though ignorance.' Despite this local resistance from a man of the cloth Hopkins still planned to go ahead and visit the town. In his letter he asked the magistrate if he would be 'welcomed and entertained.' If not the witchfinder said he would go elsewhere where he would be welcomed by 'God-fearing folk' (Haining 1974:176). Few people turned Hopkins away in case they too came under suspicion.

An entry in *The Assembly Book of Great Yarmouth* in Suffolk for August 15th 1645 recorded that the town council had agreed that 'the gentleman Mr Hopkins, employed for discovering and finding out witches, be sent for to the town to search for such wicked persons, if any be, and have his fee and allowance for his pains, as he hath in other places.' In the same year at Aldeburgh on the Suffolk coast the town chamberlain's financial accounts recorded that Hopkins was paid the sum of two pounds sterling for 'finding out witches'. One of his female assistants, Goody Phillips, was also paid one pound for her services. Several local men hired by the witchfinder during his visit to 'watch' suspected witches were paid a total of thirteen shillings and ten pennies by the town council for their help. Hunting witches appeared to be a profitable business.

However Robin Briggs believes that Matthew Hopkins was not motivated by financial rewards as many of his critics claimed. This was because Briggs claims that the fee that he charged for his services was comparatively modest. The fear of the power of witchcraft was so strong in the rural areas of eastern England at the time that Hopkins could have charged much more. Briggs says that the witch-hunter's real motivation was a mixture of an unhealthy obsession since an early age with witches and witchcraft and an egotistical satisfaction obtained from playing a role of authority when the political and legal system had virtually broken down because of the civil war (1997:191–192).

Hopkins drew up a list of rules to be used when considering the guilt of a suspected witch, some of which were based on those outlined in King James I's late 16th century treatise on witchcraft *Demonologia*. The first rule was that if only a person having a fit can see an apparition then they must have made a pact with the Devil. Suspected witches should be asked to recite the Lord's Prayer and if they failed they were automatically guilty. Evidence given by children and known criminals and convicts was to be allowed in court and a limited amount of physical violence could be used to extract confessions. Unlike the extreme methods of torture used by the European witch-hunters, which often led to the death of the victim, as mentioned earlier this was restricted to sleep deprivation, lack of food and 'walking' the suspect up and down until they collapsed from exhaustion.

Prisoners were also 'watched' by Hopkins and his assistants to see if they were visited by their imps or familiars during their confinement. These entities were said to be able to take the form of cats, dogs, rodents, insects, small birds, lizards, toads and frogs, and moles. The houses of suspects were also to be searched after their arrest for physical evidence. This included magical objects they used in their art and vessels in which they kept their familiars. Finally it was accepted that the bad character, behavior or activities of the witch's relatives or ancestors could be taken into account as reasonable grounds for suspicion.

One of the popular methods used to extract confessions was by 'swimming' or 'skimming and floating on the water.' This was an ancient concept going back to Babylonia, but was introduced into England by King James I, who already knew it in his native Scotland when he ruled that country. In his *Daemonologie* the king said water would not receive those who had 'shaken off them the Sacred Water of Baptism and willfully refuse the benefit thereof.' One of the first English instances of its use was during the examination of a suspected witch called Mother Sutton, a widow who worked as a village pigherd and lived at Milton in Bedfordshire. The woman and her daughter Mary were accused of 'devillish practices' and bewitching animals belonging to a 'gentleman of worship' (either a minister or preacher or a pious layman) called Master Enger.

Enger was encouraged by a friend of his visiting 'from the north' (possibly Scotland) to use a method of finding the women's guilt known where he lived as 'swimming'. Sutton's daughter was seized by Enger's men from the fields where she was working for a local farmer. She was taken to a watermill that was owned by her accuser and her smock was torn off. A rope was tied around her waist and her arms bound crosswise. The men then threw the terrified woman into the millpond to see if she floated and was therefore guilty. At first she sank about two feet below the surface of the water and then bobbed up and 'floated upon the water like a plank.'

Mary Sutton was dragged from the pond using the rope attached to her body. Enger then had her naked body searched by some local women for the Devil's Mark. They reported that the alleged witch had an extra nipple on her left thigh. Her illegitimate son Henry then told Enger that it was where his mother suckled her familiars in the shape of a cat and a mole. The woman was thrown back into the millpond, this time with her thumbs tied to her toes. This time she allegedly sat on top of the water, refusing to sink and turning around 'like a cartwheel' despite the strenuous efforts of Enger's men to make her sink.

As far as Master Enger was concerned his Scottish friend was right and this was sure proof that Mary Sutton was a witch. She was dragged from the water again and he closely questioned her about the bewitching of his herd of cattle and manservant and the recent death of his son. At first Sutton denied any knowledge or involvement in these incidents until Enger informed her that her own son had witnessed against her. At this news the suspected witch confessed all and both her and her mother were formally arrested. They were taken to Bedford Prison, tried and when found guilty were executed by hanging for their 'lewd and wicked practices' (Rosen 1969:333–343).

Matthew Hopkins officially began his witch-hunting activities in March 1645 and the first trial he was involved in opened at Chelmsford assizes in July of that year. It was presided over not by a proper judge, but by the Earl of Warwick. He later became the Grand Admiral of the Parliamentary Navy and his grandson married Oliver Cromwell's daughter. Nearly forty people were arraigned on witchcraft charges and Hopkins had amassed evidence against them from nearly a hundred witnesses to prove his case. Although he claimed that as a result of this first effort twenty-nine people were condemned to death, the actual figure was nearer sixteen, with two of the accused dying in custody because of the dreadful conditions in the local jail.

Matthew Hopkins, flanked by witches naming their familiars. From the witchfinder's *Discovery of Witches*, 1647.

One of the earliest cases Hopkins investigated involved a Manning-tree tailor, John Rivet. His wife had been suffering from fits for some time and no natural cause could be found to explain them. However Rivet told his friends and family that he believed she had been bewitched. The previous summer his son had died after a mysterious illness and the tailor believed there was a connection with his wife's malady. At this period all illnesses were largely regard as 'mysterious' as nobody knew their causes. He decided to consult a cunning woman at Hadleigh and she told Rivet two of his female neighbors were responsible.

Although the wise woman did not name the culprits, John Rivet decided that two local women were the ones she meant. One was called Rebecca West and the other was a 'toothless, one-legged crone', Elizabeth 'Bessie' Clark, commonly known as Old Mother Clarke. Rivet suspected that the older woman was the ringleader of the magical plot against his dead son and sick wife. This was because she had a reputation as 'an evil woman'. Also Rebecca West's mother, Anne, had been tried at the Lent Assizes of 1641 at Chelmsford for bewitching a hog to death. She was acquitted but when Matthew Hopkins got involved in the Rivet case he seized upon the incident as evidence that her daughter was a hereditary witch.

Hopkins discovered that there had been a feud between Anne West and her daughter and a family called Hart over the alleged bewitched pig. A witness, John Edes, who was possibly one of Hopkins' associates or informers in the witch-hunting business, testified that the daughter Rebecca West had told him she was visited by the Devil in the form of a young man. She had sexual relations with him and in exchange he gave her a familiar spirit in the shape of a hunting hound. She said that the Devil had promised her revenge against the Harts because of what had happened to her mother. However she must deny the Christian god and agree to serve him instead. West agreed and shortly afterwards a member of the family, John Hart, became sick and died. After that demonstration of his supernatural power, West told Edes, she firmly believed that the young man who was her new master the Devil 'could do like God.'

Hopkins had taken the unusual step of personally visiting Rebecca West several times in the spring of 1645 while she was incarnated in Colchester Castle awaiting trial. On these visits he claimed that he had tried to persuade her to denounce her mother as one of a local coven of five witches led by Old Mother Clarke. On his last visit West told

Hopkins that her mother had taken her to Clarke's house in Manning-tree where several other women and the Devil were present. She also confessed that she had married the 'young man' and had 'lain carnally' with him in her bed, even though his body was 'as cold as clay.'

However when the case came to court Rebecca West was acquitted of practicing witchcraft and having sexual intercourse with the Devil. Craig Cabell has suggested that in fact Hopkins had an ulterior motive for visiting the young woman in jail. He may have seduced her during his visits and then arranged for her acquittal when she promised to help convict the other defendants. Even the witchfinder's assistant John Stearne was surprised at the effort his master had exerted to keep the girl from being hanged with the rest of the alleged coven. He obviously regarded it as suspicious and from past experiences probably knew the reason. (Cabell 2006:27–34).

Matthew Hopkins and his company moved their operations from Essex to the neighboring county of Suffolk. John Stearne described how the witches that were subsequently executed at Edmundsbury or Bury St Edmunds in August 1645 were bodily searched. They were each found to have extra 'teats or dugs which their imps used to suck.' Most of these supernumerary nipples were discovered in the genital area of the female suspects. Richard Deacon has suggested that what the sexually ignorant searchers had found was in fact an over-developed clitoris possessed by the women (1976:111).

During the Suffolk witch-hunt Hopkins employed a new technique to try and discover if supposed witches were guilty. He had them weighed against the local church Bible. If they were lighter than the book then it was offered as evidence they were guilty as charged. In the 17th century many church Bibles were not only heavy books, they were also fixed with solid metal clasps, locks and chains. The accused female 'witch' was often small, thin and malnourished and therefore the books would always weigh heavier then they did and in Hopkins' prejudiced view this indicated their obvious guilt.

The victims of the East Anglian witch-hunt were not always from the poor rural peasant class. There is one reference to a parson's wife who was described as 'a gentle-woman of a very godly and religious life.' In her cases the charges were eventually dropped. Less lucky was Henry Carre of Rattlesden. He was described as a 'well educated man' and a Cambridge scholar. It is possible that because he had a good education Carre challenged the threats from the witchfinder and refused to confess his guilt. John Stearne claimed that he personally examined Carre and found 'marks on him'. He was also supposed to have possessed two imps in the shape of 'hairy mice.' Carre died in prison before he came to trial and would probably have been acquitted. Mother Lakeland, executed for witchcraft at Ipswich in 1645, was said to have good social connections. She was described as a 'godly and reputable woman.'

One of the other respectable people with high social status that Hopkins moved against was the Reverend John Lewes or Lowes, the vicar of the parish of Brandeston in Suffolk appointed in 1596. He was a graduate of St John's College, Cambridge and had gained a reputation as a dissident, non-conformist and troublemaker. In the early years of his appointment Lowes became involved in numerous legal disputes and arguments with his parishioners and neighbors. He was hauled before the bishop's court in Ipswich and charged with not conforming to the rites and rituals of the established Church. It was even alleged at the hearing that he had secret pro-Catholic sympathies. Shortly afterwards the clergyman was convicted of 'maliciously inciting litigation.'

It has even been said that Lowes had been charged with practicing witchcraft (Summers 1928). In 1615 a man claimed the cleric had bewitched his daughter and sent his imps to his house and they had threatened to kill him. Witnesses claimed the vicar had caused illnesses to afflict village children, attempted to poison the son of 'a local gentleman' (wealthy landowner) and bewitched livestock. He had also helped a known witch and had hidden her in his house from pursuers. In his spirited defense Lowes vehemently denied the charges. He claimed he had spent fifteen years trying to reform his ignorant and 'vice ridden flock' without success. As a result they were now conspiring against him to remove his living as a minister.

The Reverend Lowes seems to have survived these charges, but in 1642 he appeared in an anonymous broadsheet called *A Magazine of Scandall*. He was described as a 'disturber of the peace', a braggart, a royalist, a Catholic sympathizer and a wizard. Lowes had spent many years preaching vindictive 'fire and brimstone' sermons against his parishioners. Because they had been unable to remove the clergyman from office despite all his alleged crimes, it is evident that the villagers hatched a new plot to accuse the troublesome priest of practicing witchcraft. This time they had Matthew Hopkins on hand to do their dirty work.

When Hopkins visited Brandeston in 1645 looking for witches he was already aware of the long running dispute between its inhabitants and the vicar. He found no shortage of witnesses who did not like Lowes and were willing to accuse him of witchcraft. One man said he had an argument with the clergyman who threatened him with physical violence. The man had sought a legal warrant 'to bind him to the peace' or restrain him. Shortly afterwards Lowes, possibly in a gesture of reconciliation, gave the man's wife some money for her son. When the child became ill and died the couple pointed the finger of suspicion at Lowes and said he had bewitched their son with charmed coins.

When he was arrested Lowes at first denied all the charges against him. To try and force a confession from the eighty-year-old man he was beaten, starved and deprived of sleep for several nights. He was then forced to run up and down, backwards and forwards, until he was out of breath and gasping for air. This went on continuously for both days and nights until he began to tell his torturers what they wanted to hear. Lowes confessed to owning seven imps including a yellow one that he used to sink ships at the port of Yarmouth. This same familiar had also been responsible for the death of many cattle. The cleric said that he had gone to a village near Harwich to preach the gospel. As he was taking a walk along the sea wall he had seen a fleet of ships go past. He had sent his imp to sink a new vessel in the middle of the fleet and it sank under the waves. He also told his questioners he had made a pact with the Devil and signed the document in his own blood.

When the Reverend Lowes was finally brought to trial he told the court he was innocent and repudiated the confessions he had made under duress. Despite this plea he was found guilty as charged and sentenced to be hanged. Lowes insisted on having a Christian funeral service and burial as convicted witches were interred in unconsecrated ground. Even as he walked to the gallows he was still protesting his innocence. After the vicar was hanged some people said he had only been persecuted and killed because he had been a troublemaker and Catholic sympathizer. As a result Lowes became something of a martyr and a whispering campaign began against Hopkins and his gang. Richard Deacon suggested that this marked the beginning of the end of the witchfinder's career even though many more victims were destined to die in the next two years (1976:152).

Matthew Hopkins traveled to Norfolk in the autumn of 1645 as he had heard from his informers that there were many witches in the county. He had also been invited by the local authorities to deal with the witchcraft problem. At Great Yarmouth thirteen people were charged from September to December with bewitching, using witchcraft to find lost money and entertaining evil spirits. Three were acquitted, seven were hanged, one was reprieved but probably executed later and the fate of the others is unknown.

Typical of the cases that were tried in Norfolk was that of a spinster called Elizabeth Bradwell who was charged with bewitching two people and hanged. Bradwell had gone to see a hosier, a dealer in woven or knitted woolen stockings and underclothes, called Henry Moulton seeking work. His maid told her that her employer was not available and sent her away. Bradwell left the premises in an angry mood. That night she was visited by a 'tall black man'. He cut her hand with a knife and told her to write her name in blood in a black book. He then gave Bradwell a bag full of gold coins and promised he would help her get revenge on the hosier. However in return she had to agree to serve him for the rest of her life. She eagerly agreed to the deal. Possibly this dark stranger was the local witch-master who had heard about the incident and took the opportunity to recruit Bradwell.

The next night the Man in Black visited Bradwell bearing some bad news. He told her he could not harm Moulton because he was a devout man who attended church and said his prayers before retiring each night. Instead Bradwell decided to target Moulton's young child with her own newly acquired magical powers. The Man in Black made a wax image to represent the child and told Bradwell to bury it in a churchyard. Following this action she got her revenge as the child became sick and died.

From Norfolk Hopkins passed into Huntingdonshire and began his campaign there in the spring of 1646. Suspected witches were forced to sit on a low wooden stool placed in the middle of the room. They had to sit cross-legged in an uncomfortable position for hours until they temporarily lost the use of their legs. If they did not voluntarily submit to this treatment they were forcibly tied to the stool with ropes. The suspect was kept in this position for twenty-four hours without food and drink or sleep. During this period the Watchers employed by Hopkins observed the suspect to see if they were visited by their familiars. Even the appearance of spiders, flies or fleas in the cell was regarded as evidence they had imps. At this time most prisons were infested with vermin including insects, mice and rats. As a result of this treatment confessions were obtained from nine alleged witches, male and female, and they were tried and hanged.

In the late spring and early summer of 1647 Matthew Hopkins and John Stearne had extended their witch-hunting activities to the Cambridgeshire fenlands and the ancient Isle of Ely, long associated with witchcraft. Ely had always had a bad reputation since the Middle Ages as the habitat of 'rude uncivil inbreds.' The town was frequently cut off from the outside world by floodwaters in the winter and at the high spring tides. Its uneducated, illiterate inhabitants mostly made a living by cutting reeds for thatching houses, digging peat to sell as fuel and catching eels and wildfowl for resale. Many of them were highly superstitious. Around the hearth at night they told stories of local witches and any misfortune or bad luck they suffered was blamed on their magical powers or the faeries and demonic powers of darkness lurking in the surrounding fens.

As a result of Hopkins' activities in the area a total of fourteen people, three of them men, were arrested. Seven were later hanged. In one case a woman from Ely had the charges against her dropped when she agreed to become of the witchfinder's many informers. This woman may have been the same one Hopkins had sent into the fens in early 1647 as a spy. He told her to pretend she was looking for a husband and use this cover to find out if any witches were operating in the area. 'White witches' and cunning women often acted as marriage brokers or were consulted to reveal the identity of future husbands or lovers. Often they prescribed love potions or charms. Hopkins also had an aunt living in Ely and it is possible she supplied him with intelligence about witchcraft.

At the beginning of 1647 the tide of public opinion was turning against Hopkins and his gang and they were being criticized for their activities and methods. As early as 1645 when Hopkins began his campaign of terror a Parliamentary Commission was set up to examine the confessions he had extracted from prisoners. They condemned the practice of 'swimming' alleged witches, although their attempts to outlaw the practice failed (Davies 1999:89). However the head of the Commission told Hopkins that he could not 'swim' suspects without their permission. They were to be given the choice of being 'swam' as a way of proving their innocence. Given that choice few would have taken it. As result of these comments Hopkins did suspend the practice for a year. However the other methods of interrogation for obtaining confessions that bordered on torture continued.

Hopkins' assistant John Stearne complained that in one town the witch-hunters visited there was organized opposition to the arrest of one suspected witch. Two unnamed men publicly campaigned to stop the trial and threatened Stearne and the witnesses he had gathered with violence. The woman was eventually tried and condemned to death. However she was reprieved due to the efforts of her chief defender. In another case Stearne was issued with a writ accusing him of taking part in a conspiracy to hunt down alleged witches in the Essex town of Colchester. He identified the person responsible for the legal challenge as a local merchant who believed his business was being threatened by the witch-hunters' activities (MacFarlane 1970:138–139).

One of Hopkins most vociferous critics was an East Anglian clergyman called John Gaule of Great Staughton in Huntingdonshire. While he believed in the existence of witches and the power of witchcraft, he disagreed with the Witchfinder-General's methods of hunting them down and securing convictions. Liberally he also believed some of those arrested and executed were innocent. In June 1646 Gaule published a small booklet containing as series of sermons he had preached on the subject of witchcraft in a four-week period. In it he claimed that the death of many alleged witches had been 'wrongly caused by the malice and imposture of one Matthew Hopkins.' He further described him as 'nothing but a charlatan and a nuisance.' Gaule claimed the activities of the witch-hunter and his gang had encouraged popular superstition, divided communities, increased the suffering of the poor and was an insult to justice and the rule of the law.

Hopkins reacted swiftly and badly to this criticism from a respected cleric of the Church who he hoped would have supported his anti-witchcraft crusade. He privately published his own booklet *The Discoverie of Witches in Answer to Several Queries* using a printing company in London. In it he defended his methods of seeking out witches. By using what he thought were reasoned arguments Hopkins believed he could counter the criticism and especially the allegation that he had made a rich living from witch-finding. Evidently he failed in his mission as in 1647 he suddenly vanished from the public eye.

One allegation persistently made against Hopkins was that he himself was a sorcerer or wizard who used his powers to find practitioners of witchcraft. Many of the cunning folk acted as amateur witchfinders and Hopkins was known to be a friend of the famous astrologer William Lilly. As was seen earlier, they may have first met when Hopkins worked as a shipping clerk for a maritime insurance company. Lilly was a regular visitor to Essex and is known to have stayed at the Thorn Inn at Mistley. This public house was either owned by Hopkins or he had some financial interest in the property, which he used as the headquarters for his activities.

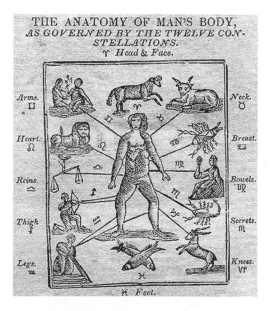

Early modern astrological almanac, of the type in use by cunning folk.

William Lilly had been born in Leicestershire, the son of a yeoman, and began practicing astrology in 1641. Although outwardly he supported the Cromwellian faction in the civil war, like others caught up in the conflict he backed both sides and it is said gave astrological advice to the royalists. Lilly is supposed to have offered his services to Hopkins several times 'on various matters relating to shippes and cargoes, as well as some darker aspects of the signes of the time apertayning to witchcraft.' One of Hopkins' informants, William Hills, had been taught astrology by Lilly and ironically, and perhaps hypocritically, used his knowledge to recover stolen goods.

Lilly was supposed to have been consulted by the Parliamentary forces despite their deeply held religious views. Richard Deacon says he was involved in what intelligence services today describe as psychological warfare (1976:70). During the siege of Colchester he was sent to tell the army outside the town that he predicted it would soon fall to them. He also seems to have been involved in detecting witches and his casebooks contain no less than forty references to witchcraft. This may explain the astrologer's frequent visits to the notorious 'witch country' of Essex and his friendship with Matthew Hopkins.

Another lodger at the Thorn Inn was John Thurlowe, the son of an Essex clergyman who had been appointed by Oliver Cromwell as the chief of his secret service. As a young man he had studied law and it is possible that is how he first met Hopkins. Lilly knew and had worked for Thurlowe, although he was possibly a double-agent who also paid by the royalists for information and astrological advice. Thurlowe also had a keen interest in witchcraft and was reported to have investigated secret papists and the magical rituals and sex orgies held at Sir William Maxie's house in 1643 mentioned earlier.

Richard Deacon speculated that Matthew Hopkins was a secret agent working for Thurlowe. His witch-hunting activities were merely a useful cover for discovering and disposing royalist sympathizers and spies in eastern England. Cabell says that William Lilly provided Hopkins with some information on 'occult letters.' This was a 'Rosicrucian cipher' used by Thurlowe's agents and also Hopkins' informers to communicate. It was also used to identify the houses of known royalists and suspected witches by writing the code on the wall. Some of the witches were believed by Thurlowe to be royalists agents who supported the king. A contemporary source also claimed that there was a clandestine group of royalists in East Anglia intent on protecting those attacked by Hopkins and his gang (Deacon 1976:187). In 1643 a woman from Newbury in Berkshire was accused at her trial for witchcraft of spying on a local troop of the New Model Army with the intention of having it destroyed.

The cipher used by Thurlowe and Hopkins was named after the medieval occult secret society known by its full title as the *Fraterniti Rosa Crux* or the Fraternity of the Rosy Cross. As well as its use by secret agents, the Rosicrucian cipher was supposedly also employed by cunning men in Essex for magical purposes. According to Richard Deacon, who also wrote books on intelligence matters under another pen-name, the cipher was still being used in the 19th century by the famous cunning man James Murrell, who died in 1860. After his death his son found a codebook containing the cipher among the books in his father's magical library. Allegedly the book had been inherited by Murrell from a 17th century wizard who used the pseudonym Neoboad. His handwriting was so small and crabbed that a magnifying glass had to be used to read it.

Richard Deacon quotes an example of some writings in the Rosicrucian cipher that refer to Neoboad as a 'master of witches'—a term given to a cunning man who controlled the local witches in his area and may possibly have been their 'man in black' or worldly representative of the Devil. It says that Neoboad had come across a cunning woman from the Essex village of Hadleigh called Mistress Hoy who had broken the spells of 'the good angels...Raphael, Adonai [in fact a Hebrew name for God] and Ephraim'. The extract in code also refers to one of Hopkin's victims, Elizabeth Clarke, and to the casting of a horoscope for King Charles I.

Deacon claims that the coded extract suggests that a mysterious personage known as by the cover name of Neoboad controlled or supervised witches in Essex who had royalist sympathies. Apparently the coven had been betrayed by the cunning woman from Hadleigh and as a result Elizabeth Clarke was arrested. (1976:191). At her trial in 1645, one of the first Hopkins had been involved in, John Rivet had said he had consulted a wise woman from Hadleigh called Hoy. She had named Clarke as one of those responsible for cursing his wife.

As an interesting sidelight on the claim that Hopkins was a warlock or cunning man is an article written by the founder of modern Wicca, Gerald B. Gardner, and published in the June 1939 edition of *Folk-lore*, the journal of the Folklore Society. In it Gardner claimed he had obtained a wooden box that allegedly contained several items of a magical nature that had once belonged to Matthew Hopkins. The box had been given to Gardner by an unknown person who knew of his interest in the history of witchcraft.

The outside of the box had a 19th century paper label on it that read: 'This talisman [sic] made and sold by Matthew Hopkins...was given to my father Joseph Carter of Home Farm, Hill Top, nr Marlborough [Wiltshire] and contains the finger of Mary Holt, the notorious Wiltshire witch [signed] S. Carter.' Inside the box were some dried wild flowers, a twig [wood unidentified] shaped like a cockerel's claw, some bits of tree bark, a hawthorn twig covered in moss, a [human?] bone with skin attached, a bird [unidentified], a scrap of parchment with the words 'Matthew Hopkins talisman against all witch-crafts' written on it in modern lettering, a small wax image of a head with hair attached [possibly the remains of a poppet or wax image used for cursing], a Seal of Solomon [six pointed star] made from lead, and a human finger bone, presumably belonging to the Wiltshire witch mentioned on the label.

Gerald Gardner also had another object that had alleged belonged to the Witchfinder-General. It was a small baton or wand measuring twelve and a half inches in length. It was surmounted by an equal-armed cross made from bone, again possibly of either animal or human origin. Attached to this object was a tattered paper label in the same handwriting as the one with the box saying it was 'Matthew Hopkins sceptre or tutti stick [sic] It added that it had been used by the witch-finder 'during his travels in the south of England [sic], finding and exposing witches.'

If these items were genuine and had really belonged to Hopkins it is evidence that he was either using magical techniques to find witches or made extra money selling talismans or amulets to people who believed they were victims of bewitchment. It adds some credence to the story that Hopkins was himself accused of practicing witchcraft and 'swam' by a mob to make him confess. After this he suddenly gave up his witch-finding activities. One writer called Samuel Butler claimed that Hopkins 'made a rod for his own breeches' and 'after prov'd himself a witch' and another source said he had 'died miserably' in unknown circumstances. In his book *Bygone Essex* (1892) the pioneering folklorist William Andrews claimed that while Hopkins was staying in Suffolk a mob accused him of being in league with the Devil. They said he owned a 'Black Book' (the name used for the home-made handwritten grimoires or grammers of magic used by cunning folk) listing all the witches in England and had acquired it through sorcery. This was why he was successful in finding witches. Allegedly Hopkins was tied hand to foot and thrown into a river to see if he floated.

Another version of the same story said the 'swimming' of Hopkins happened near the Thorn Inn at Mistley and he was thrown in the village pond. The account continues by saying that when the witchfinder floated on the surface of the river, possibly buoyed up by air trapped in his clothing, he was dragged out and either lynched by the mob on the spot or died shortly afterwards from a chill. Allegedly his body was buried secretly at night in an unmarked grave 'outside the churchyard', i.e., in unconsecrated ground where suspected witches were interred.

Yet another tale that circulated in the villages of East Anglia claimed that Hopkins fled the country altogether when people turned against him. He allegedly caught a ship to America, where his brother Thomas had emigrated some years earlier to the New England. The American colonies also had their fanatical Puritans, cunning folk and witch-hunts of course. Hopkins activities were known to the colonists as during the trial of the infamous Salem witches the prosecutor Cotton Mather made a reference to the witch-hunts back in England.

Some people said that the reason Hopkins suddenly disappeared was because he had been exposed as a double-agent secretly working for the royalist army. This theory came about because of Hopkins' odd relationship with Lady Jane Whorwood. She was a prominent royalist aristocrat who in 1648 was behind a plot to rescue King Charles I from prison before he was beheaded the following year. Coincidentally she was also an associate of the astrologer William Lilly. He had advised Lady Jane that the position of the planets indicated that the best place for the king to hide after his escape was in Essex where he would get 'a warm welcome' from pro-royalist factions.

Whatever happened to Matthew Hopkins he gave up his witch-hunting career in late 1647 or early 1648. John Stearne had also abandoned his role as a witch-hunter, had left Manningtree and moved over the border into Suffolk to a village six miles south of Bury St Edmund. Stearne refuted the wild and fanciful stories that his former employer had been 'swum' as a witch. Instead there was no mystery and he claimed that Hopkins had died peacefully in his hometown of Manningtree probably sometime in 1648. The cause of his demise was consumption or tuberculosis, which apparently he had been suffering from for many years.

Matthew Hopkins seems to have survived death if stories of sightings of his restless ghost can be believed. In 1974 the local newspaper, the *Harwich & Manningtree Standard*, published a story saying that the church at Mistley was believed to be haunted by the spectre of a man said to be the Witchfinder-General. The attic at the old Thorn Inn was also the scene of sightings of his ghost. In Manningtree an occupant of an old house in South Street where Hopkins once lived reported a resident apparition in old-fashioned clothing. It was often seen walking in through the front door and went out by the back door. The leader of the Mistley Spiritualist Circle was quoted in the newspaper as saying that the Red Lion Inn at Manningtree, which he frequented when he was alive, was haunted by Hopkins. A séance was held in the public house in 1969 and a clairvoyant claimed to have seen a spirit wearing dark clothing. It was hatless, holding a cane, with dank, oily hair and dark glittering eyes. She said the hostile apparition stared hard at the sitters at the séance before vanishing into thin air.

Some years ago allegedly Hopkins, or at least his ghostly voice speaking through a medium, made an appearance on a cable television program featuring real-life haunted places. It was presented by a famous psychic who held a recorded séance in the churchyard of St Nicholas at the infamous 'witch village' of Canewdon on the Essex marshes. During the program the team had a spirit communication from an entity who claimed to be the Witchfinder-General Matthew Hopkins. The local cunning man Old George Pickingill is buried in the churchyard so perhaps the spirit of Hopkins was looking for him.

4

Imps and Familiars

MOST OF THE confessions extracted by Matthew Hopkins from alleged witches and the testimony of witnesses feature stories about familiar spirits. In fact the familiar is a very English phenomenon. According to popular witch beliefs when a person was initiated by the Devil or the 'Man in Black' among the gifts he gave him or her was a familiar spirit or imp (a 'child of the Devil' or 'little devil'). One of its tasks was to act as a messenger and link between the witch and her dark master. It was also 'sent forth' by the witch to cause injury or death to her enemies. Sometimes the familiar appeared as a human being and the Scottish witch Bessie Dunlop had one who was a man killed in a past battle who wore old-fashioned clothes of the period. When in human form the familiar was similar to the spirit guides known to modern Spiritualist mediums. Usually though the familiar took the form of a small animal that the witch could easily explain away as a domestic pet, even if some of them were unusual and exotic in nature.

Although the term 'familiar' meaning a minor demon attending a witch was not used widely until the 16th century, there are references to the concept some four hundred years earlier. In the 12th century Lady Rosamund Clifford, often called 'Fair Rosamund' or, in a pun on the Latin version of her name, 'Rose of the World' (from *Rosa Mundi*), was the mistress of King Henry II who reigned from 1154–1189. Henry ruled over a vast kingdom that covered England, Wales, Ireland, Normandy and Brittany in northern France, and the French provinces of Anjou and Aquitaine. His wife Eleanor of Aquitaine has been described as one of the dynamic and powerful women in medieval Europe.

Rosamund was the daughter of Lord Walter de Clifford and she first met King Henry when he stayed at her father's castle on the Welsh border with England. The king and his army were on their way into Wales to put down a rebellion by the Welsh prince Rhys ap Gruffyd. The king took an immediate fancy to the beautiful, young and unmarried Rosamund. They immediately began an intense and clandestine love affair that was to eventually end in tragedy. Henry was supposed to have built a special bower for Rosamund in the garden of his palace at Woodstock in Oxfordshire. He surrounded it with a hedge labyrinth or maze and the star-crossed lovers used it for their secret trysts behind the queen's back. Unfortunately Queen Eleanor was not only a political manipulator, she was also a very jealous woman and did not want somebody usurping her relationship to the king. When she discovered the illicit affair Eleanor plotted to kill her husband's mistress in a particularly horrible and painful way. She employed three witches to send their familiars in the form of venomous toads to kill Rosamund. They did this by biting her all over so their poison entered her blood and she died in agony.

When and where the idea of witches' familiars arose in accounts of English witchcraft is unknown. However both the Tudor and Jacobean Witchcraft Acts mentioned the summoning and entertaining of spirits. The 17th century critic of the witch-hunting hysteria, Thomas Ady, said it should not be unlawful for anyone to keep a rat, mouse, dormouse, rabbit, bird, grasshopper or snake. If they did they should not be accused of witchcraft and of having a familiar spirit. He referred to an 'honest woman' who was executed in Cambridge in 1645 because she kept a tame frog for 'sport and phantasie' and the judge decided it was her familiar and evidence she practised witchcraft.

C. L'Estrange Ewen believed that the concept of the familiar spirit probably originated in the habit of socially isolated and lonely women, spinsters and widows, keeping pets for company. As they were scorned by their neighbors these social outsiders instead made a substitute relationship with a dog or cat. It is something that is not unknown today. The problems arose when the women decided to keep more unusual pets such as ferrets, rats, mice, lizards or toads. Then they left themselves open to accusations of witchcraft and illegally owning and entertaining familiar spirits (1933).

One classic example of a favorite pet belonging to a famous person that superstitious people and his enemies believed was a familiar was

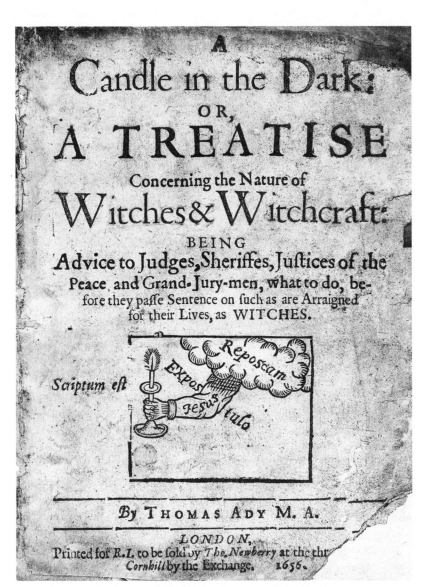

A
Candle in the Dark:
OR,
A TREATISE
Concerning the Nature of
Witches & Witchcraft:
BEING
Advice to Judges, Sheriffes, Justices of the
Peace, and Grand-Jury-men, what to do, before they passe Sentence on such as are Arraigned
for their Lives, as WITCHES.

Scriptum est

Repostam
Expos tulo
Jesus

By THOMAS ADY M. A.

LONDON,
Printed for *R. I.* to be sold by *Tho. Newberry* at the thr
Cornhill by the Exchange. 1656.

Title page of the 1656 edition of Thomas Ady's *A Candle in the Dark*.

mentioned in the chapter on Matthew Hopkins. King Charles I's colorful German nephew, Prince Rupert of the Rhine (1619–1682), was a noted soldier, scientist and artist. At the young age of twenty-three his uncle appointed the prince as the commanding general of the royalist cavalry in the civil war against the Roundheads. Rupert had a devoted white dog called 'Boyo' that followed him everywhere. During military planning meetings the dog sat beside its master and he would frequently kiss the animal. The intimate relationship between Prince Rupert and Boyo led to some people hinting that it was unnatural.

Rumors began to circulate from the Puritan side that Rupert was a wizard and the dog was his familiar with supernatural powers. In 1643 an anonymous pamphlet claimed the dog was like a cunning man and had the power of prophecy, could locate lost or stolen goods, make itself invisible, talk and protect its master from being harmed in battle by magical means. Although it was German the animal was said to come from Lappland (modern Finland) 'where none but devils and sorcerers live.' In popular lore the Lapps were regarded as natural magicians and the area was regarded as a center for teaching witchcraft and the magical arts.

In 1644 Boyo was hit by a musket ball during the Battle of Marston Moor and died. Possibly it had been singled out by a Roundhead marksman. A Puritan writer penned a satirical poem in the dog's honor in which the dead poodle was described as a 'valiant souldier, who had skille in Necromancie.' The tongue-in-cheek poem went on to say the 'malignant whelp' had been revered by witches, the pope and the Devil. It advised the royalist cavaliers to lament his loss as the dog could no longer protect their 'dammes' (wives or lady friends) or provide them with victory in battle.

Richard Barnard, the author of the influential *A Guide To Grand Jury-Man* (1627) stated, 'witches have ordinarily a familiar or spirit, in the shape of a Man, Woman, Boy, Dog, Cat, Foal, Fowl, Hare, Rat, Toad etc. And to these spirits they give names, and they meet together to Christen them.' Other animal forms taken by familiars were weasels, ferrets, polecats (a small carnivorous mammal of the weasel family similar to the American skunk), white rabbits, white mice and moles, insects such as butterflies and moths, and birds such as cormorants, seagulls, crows, ravens, magpies and owls. While it is popularly believed that feline familiars were black in fact the true witch's cat was a brindle one. That is, one with brownish or tawny fur and streaks of other colors.

The fact that the familiar was often an ordinary pet was proved by Dr William Harvey, the personal physician of King Charles II (reigned 1649–1685). The doctor was visiting Newmarket in Suffolk and heard stories about a reputed witch living in the town. He arranged to visit the woman pretending to be a wizard and gained her confidence. Dr Harvey asked the witch if it was possible to see her familiar spirit and she agreed to his request. Making a weird chuckling sound, the woman showed the doctor a toad she kept inside a wooden chest. She then proceeded to feed it with a saucer of fresh milk. The doctor persuaded her to leave the house and run an errand for him. While she was out Harvey seized the toad and sliced it open using the dissecting knife he always carried in his bag. By this cruel act the physician established that the amphibian was no different from any other one and there was nothing supernatural about it (*Gentleman's Magazine* 1832). What the witch said or did when she returned and found her pet had been butchered is not recorded.

In the accounts of the witch trials the familiar did not always take the shape of a human or animal. Sometimes it was less material and took on an intangible and spiritual form. For instance a male witch from Ely, Adam Sobie, accused in 1647, said his familiar took the form of a 'flame of fire', suggesting it may have been an elemental. The Huntingdonshire witch Lizzie Weed described how her familiar materialized in her bed chamber in the dark. It asked her to seal their covenant by signing it in her blood and Weed did so 'by the light of the spirit' itself to see by (Ewen 1933:221).

Occasionally the familiar had a composite or hybrid form taking the physical characteristics of several different animals or looked like no known earthly beast. One Suffolk example called Vinegar Tom was described by Matthew Hopkins as having the body and legs of a dog and the head of an ox with horns. At the trial of the St Osyth witches in 1582 Anne Herd said she had six familiars that looked like cows but were the size of rats. They were colored red and white, traditionally the colors associated with Otherworldly faery animals such as cattle and dogs. They are described in folklore as being white with red ears.

When the Devil or his human representative the Man in Black gave a familiar to a witch it usually came with a name. For instance during the Hopkins witch-hunt in Huntingdonshire in 1646 Jane Wallis was visited in her bed by 'a man in blacke cloathes' who said his name was 'Blackeman' (sic). He gave her two familiars like dogs with 'bristles on their backs resembling hogs.' The man in black told the woman she must call them Grizzell and Greediguts. If she did they were for her to command and would do or fetch anything she needed or wanted.

Other unusual names given in East Anglia to witches' familiars by either the Devil or their owner were Pyewacket, Sathan, Pusse, Robyn or Robin, Tomboy, Hangman, Mousey, Perry, Pluck, Pugge, Littleman, Tom Tit and Titty, Prickear, Pickpocket, Lift-the-Hatch, Sacke, Sugar, Beelzebub, Peck, Butterin, Mamillion, Dandy, Vizett, Hisse, Blew, Calico, Tewhit (not surprisingly for an owl familiar), Biddy and Biddy, Jack, Jill, Jockey and Neddy.

In 1645 the Suffolk witch Mother Hubbard was visited by three 'small things' who whispered to her that if she renounced her God and the Christ she would want for nothing. They told her their names were Thomas, Richard and Hobb and she should call these out to summon them. Hobb or Hob in English folklore was the name for a brownie or domestic spirit that lived in farmhouses and helped with the chores, i.e., a hobgoblin named after the hob or oven. They were associated with the nature spirit Robin Goodfellow and Robin was a name of the god of the witches. Hob was also an archaic nickname used by country folk for the Devil.

Although the familiar could come as a gift from the Old One it could also be inherited from a relative who was a practitioner of witchcraft. Alternatively it might be gifted by another witch, especially if they knew they were about to die. In 1588 an Essex witch confessed that she had three familiars: one like a cat called Lightfoot, a toad called Lunch and a weasel known as Makeshift. She said that Lightfoot had been sold to her sixteen years before by another witch, Mother Barbie. She had paid its former owner for it with some food.

As discussed before, at her trial at Chelmsford Elizabeth Francis said she had passed her inherited familiar Sathan to a neighbor. Margerie Sammon, who was one of the 16th century covine of St Osyth witches, said her mother had given her two familiars that looked like toads in a wicker basket that was half full with wool. Sammon's mother had told her that if anything happened to her she should send the familiars to another witch, Mother Pechney, for safekeeping. In this way familiars were passed from witch to witch.

Eric Maple said that in the infamous 'witch village' of Canewdon the familiars owned by the local witches usually took the form of white mice and were the source of their power. They were kept in a small wooden box and handed on to a relative before the death of their owner. Maple recounted a story of an old woman who was dying and asked for a small box to be brought to her. It was empty but when she gave a low whistle several white mice appeared from it. In another case the witch's familiars would not leave the room after she died. The local vicar then tried to exorcise the creatures with bell, book and candle. When that failed the mice were eventually caught and buried in the coffin with their previous owner (Maple 1960).

It was said that in the 19th century one blacksmith in Canewdon was a wizard and had sold his soul to the Devil in exchange for his metalwork skills. When he was at death's door his familiars appeared on his bedspread as several white mice. The smith said he wanted to 'pass on the power' and at first asked his wife to continue his legacy. When she said that she wanted nothing to do with the Black Art and refused, he turned to his daughter. She too was reluctant until her father said he could not die until he passed on his witch power. Not wanting to watch him linger in agony for days, the daughter finally agreed. She took the mice away and the smith died in peace knowing she would carry on his magical tradition (Maple 1962:187).

Mrs Eve, a contemporary of the famous Essex cunning man James Murrell, lived in an old cottage near the Wagon and Horses public house in Hadleigh. When she died the villagers were so in fear of her reputation that nobody would volunteer to lay the body out. Eventually two women agreed to do it. Just as they were finishing the task a man came to the cottage door. He introduced himself to the two layer-outs as the dead woman's son. The man said he had been working in the fields outside another village when the fetch or spirit double of his mother materialized before him. He realized that this was the witch's way of informing her son that she had died. When the man had finished work he made his way to the cottage. Mrs Eve's son seemed to be in a frightened state and he admitted to the women that he was scared. This was because he did not want to inherit his witch-mother's powers and knowledge. He then went to a drawer in an old chest, opened it and took out a wooden box. The women could see it contained some kind of live creature. To their surprise the man threw the box on the open fire. As he did a terrible screaming sound came from it. The shocked women then heard the witch's son mutter 'I am free at last!' (Morgan 1973:46)

The Witch of Lodden in Norfolk, who also lived in the 19th century, had three imps the size of rats that resembled small human beings with bat wings. She kept these strange creatures in a wooden box and if women came to her wanting to learn about witchcraft she let them out to bite their breasts. In that way they would become witches as well. Several brave women were quite willing to endure this ordeal to learn the secrets of the witch's art. One dark and stormy night the old witch lay dying. She called her only daughter into her bedroom and instructed the girl to take the box containing the familiars from its hiding place. The mother told her offspring to release the imps from their confinement. She was then to allow the creatures to bite her breasts. In that way the hereditary power of witchcraft would be passed on down the family line from the dying mother to her daughter.

When the girl did as she was told and opened the wooden box the room was filled with the sound of demonic laughter. At this the imps began squealing as if they were in pain. The witch's daughter was terrified and instinctively she threw the box and its contents into the fire. Not long after the old witch died a tall dark stranger called at the house. He made love to the daughter and took her away with him. She was never seen in the village again and people said her mysterious visitor was no ordinary man. He was in fact the Devil in human form and had claimed the daughter as his bride as part of the pact he had made with her witch-mother when she was alive (Porter 1974:148–49).

When Susan Cooper, the Witch of Whittlesford, Cambridgeshire, died in 1878 large crowds flocked to the funeral. It may have been from respect or perhaps they just wanted to make sure she was really dead. After she was buried and the funeral service had ended the children from the village school trampled on her newly dug grave. When asked by an outsider, who had attended the witch's funeral out of curiosity, why they were doing this the children told him: 'So her imps don't get out' (Porter 1969:175).

A Norfolk minister was told by one of his parishioners that an old witch had attempted to give her familiars to a young woman she had selected to be her successor. The witch handed over a small wooden box that allegedly contained the imps. Unfortunately the recipient did not want to become a witch. She was so frightened by the sound of scratching coming from the box that she burnt it (Glyde 1872:55). In all these cases the only way that the familiar spirits could be destroyed was through the purifying flames of a fire. In Scotland, where suspected witches were also hanged, their bodies were taken down from the gallows and burnt in a pyre to destroy their 'virtue' or power and to stop their spirits bothering the living.

In some of the accounts of the gifting of a familiar by the Devil to one of his disciples there is confusion as to whether it was a separate spirit or the Horned One himself taking the form of a small animal or bird. The Italian witch-hunter and demonologist Francesco Guazzo writing in 1608 said the Devil could manifest in the earthly world as a man or a woman or as a dog, cat, goat or owl. In 13th century Ireland the noblewoman Lady Alice Kyteler sacrificed cockerels to her familiar spirit called Robin Artisson or 'Robin, son of Art'. However he was also described as either the Devil or a demon who was 'one of the poorer classes of Hell.'

Whether the familiar was the Devil in bestial disguise or just a minor spirit it had the power to grant the desires or wishes of its owner. Usually, like the pact with Old Nick, this was in exchange for their body and soul. In 1589 Joan Waterhouse offered her familiar spirit the sacrifice of a cockerel. It refused it and instead demanded the woman give herself to it body and soul. Twenty years later another Essex witch Joan Prentice owned a familiar in the shape of a weasel. This spirit animal also asked her to give up her soul to it.

A Suffolk male witch, John Bysack, claimed in 1645 that his familiar had suddenly appeared outside the window of his house. It looked like a 'rugged sandy-coloured dog' and to his utter astonishment spoke to him. In a strange and unearthly hollow voice it told him to deny God (Ewen 1933:273). Another male witch, Thomas Everard, said a spirit came to him in the middle of the night while he was in bed. It was 'some thing like a rabbit', asked Everard to deny God and then scratched him under his ear, drawing blood.

Helen Clarke confessed that her familiar was a white dog called Elinanzer. It spoke to her in a gruff masculine voice and asked her to deny Jesus Christ. If she agreed to do this the spirit promised she would never want materially for anything. A Suffolk witch, Joane Ruce, had three spirits that looked like mice and had the names Touch, Pluck and Take. They told her if she denied both God and Jesus in the future she would never need to buy food or clothes as they would be supplied to her. A familiar that appeared as a polecat to another witch from Suffolk, Anne Usher said it would bring her victuals (food). Three spirits that looked like large gray rats told Ellen Shepheard of Huntingdonshire that if she made a pact with them she would have 'all happiness' (ibid: 367).

Another witch from the same county, Anne Desborough, was told by her two spirit mice called Tib and Jane that after she died they would take her soul. Ellen Greenleafe from Suffolk had a familiar like a mole. It predicted that its mistress would be arrested and charged with practicing witchcraft. If that happened Greenleafe was not to confess. If she did and was executed then the familiar would have her immortal soul. Despite threats of this type in general the relationship between the witch and her familiar was very close and intimate. In 1653 a Cambridge woman refused to denounce her familiar as an evil spirit even though she was about to be hanged as a convicted witch. She said that the spirit had been her faithful and loyal friend and companion for sixty years. For that reason she died still refusing to condemn it as a demon.

However sometimes the alleged witches did not want the familiars they were given by the Devil. One example was Elizabeth Chandler of Huntington. In 1643 she told a court she had received two familiars, Beelzebub (the name of an ancient demon that was the 'Lord of the Flies') and Trullibub. Chandler claimed she had never wanted these entities. In fact as a good Christian she had earnestly prayed to God to be rid of them.

One aspect of the symbiotic relationship between the witch and the familiar involved feeding them. One of the St Osyth witches, a Mrs Heard, fed her blackbird and rat familiars with a rich diet of wheat, barley, oats and bread and cheese washed down with water and beer. In 1602 the Cambridgeshire witch Margaret Cotton fed her chicken spirits on a gourmet diet of roasted apples and claret wine. Joan Wallis of Huntingdonshire in 1646 told her familiars she was too poor to feed them. Several times after this they brought her two or three shillings to pay for food.

Often the familiar demanded to be fed from the witch's body, either by suckling them or drawing small drops of their blood. When Margaret Sammon enquired of her witch-mother what to feed her familiars on she was told her own breast milk would suffice. However if she did not feed them enough or irregularly they would demand to 'sucke of thy bloode' (Rosen 1969:74). Drinking small amounts of the blood of their owners in a vampiric way seems to have been a very common practice for familiars. In fact the witch-hunters searched for the spot that was used solely for that purpose.

In his learned treatise *Melampronoea* (1681) Henry Hallywell, the Master of Arts at Cambridge University, attempted to answer the anti-witchcraft skeptics by putting forward a pseudo-scientific explanation for familiars needing sustenance from food and blood. He said that 'being so debauched [they] wear away by continual deflux of particles, and therefore require some nutriment to supply the place of the fugacious . [hard to keep] atoms, which is done by sucking the blood and spirits of those forlorn wretches [witches]. And no doubt but these impure evils may take as much pleasure in sucking the warm blood of men and beasts, as a cheerful and healthy constitution n drawing in the refreshing gale of pure and sincere air.' The implication was that the familiar was taking nourishment or vitality from the life force that people believed was contained in blood. The belief that blood contained the life force of a human being was an important aspect of Anglo-Saxon magic.

The primary magical use of the familiar as far as the witch-hunters were concerned was to cause harm to the people the witch sent it to. The authorities made no distinction between the witch who used her familiar to heal or the one who sent them to harm or kill. As far as the Church was concerned, in the words of Bishop John Hooper, all familiars were 'damned spirits' and 'unclean imps' originating with the Devil whether the witches used them for good or bad purposes. The Witchcraft Act of 1604 specifically stated that nobody should 'employ, feed or reward' any type of spirit 'for any intent or purposes'. This is why mere ownership of a familiar was regarded as a criminal offence punishable by death.

Frequently in the East Anglian witch trials it was claimed that witches had used their familiars to cause injuries or fatalities to human beings and animals. In 1579 Elizabeth Bennett was supposed to have sent a familiar 'like unto a lion' or a 'rugged dog' to kill some animals belonging to a local farmer she had a row with. The spirit allegedly returned from its deadly mission and told its mistress it had successfully got rid of a red and a black cow belonging to the farmer. Bennett had received her familiar after curing a neighbor who refused to give her some yeast for cooking. As soon as she cursed the woman there was 'a great noise' and the spirit appeared (Rosen 1969:140).

One of the cases brought to court by the Witchfinder-General Matthew Hopkins in 1643 featured a suspected witch called Dorothy Ellis from Brentwood, Essex. She confessed that thirty years earlier the Devil had appeared to her 'in the likenesse of a grete catte' and demanded some of her blood. This entity, whether it was the Devil or a minor daemon or demon, then took on the role of a traditional familiar. Ellis said she used it to cause harm to her enemies and those she disliked. Ellis told the spirit cat to go and bewitch the cattle belonging to a farmer called Thomas Hitchell. Shortly after it returned his animals became sick and began to slowly die one by one. The witch then sent her familiar to take away the health and life of the young daughter of a man called Thomas Salter. As a result she also died. Not content with inflicting this tragedy on the family, Ellis sent forth the spirit again to harm the dead girl's mother. When a man called John Gotobed accused Ellis of being 'an old witch' and threw stones at her, she sent her familiar out once more to cause him harm as well (Haining 1974:20).

In 1646 Frances Moore of Huntingdonshire sent her familiar Tissy in the shape of a large white cat to kill William Foster. Moore claimed that he had tried to get two of her children hanged for stealing a loaf of bread. In the 17th century any form of stealing, however petty, was punished by the death penalty. As a result of the visit by the spirit Foster became very ill. He suffered in agony for seven or eight days before finally dying (Davenport 1646:5).

In the trial of the Lowestoft witches in Suffolk in 1665 a witness called Dr Jacobs said he had been called in by a family to treat their bewitched children. The doctor told the parents to take a blanket used by the sick children and hang it up. Anything found in the blanket was to be immediately thrown into the fire. When the parents did this a small toad fell out of the folds of the blanket and they disposed of it as the doctor had ordered. When they threw it into the flames it exploded. After the person responsible for bewitching the children was found they were exposed because they had burns on their body (Briggs 1997:209). This suggests the toad was a witch's fetch or spirit double projected from their physical body. Any injury inflicted on the fetch would result in a corresponding wound appearing on the witch.

With the passing of the new Witchcraft Act in 1736 alleged witches and wizards were only taken to court if they were suspected of pretending to have magical powers or psychic abilities. Then they only faced charges of fraud and deception. However popular beliefs about witches and the power of witchcraft persisted and flourished. This led to instances of mob rule and vigilante justice against suspected witches. One of these surviving beliefs was that the witch always had a familiar spirit and it had been given to them by a relative, another witch or the Devil himself. This idea survived in rural parts of England, and especially in East Anglia, well into the 20th century. In 1795 a suspected witch from Stanningfield in Suffolk was seized from her home by an angry mob seeking revenge for her alleged crimes. They took her to the village pond next to the parish church and as in the old days 'swam' her to find out if she was guilty or not. As a result of this ordeal the old woman, the delightfully named Mrs Greygoose, confessed that she did practice witchcraft and owned six imps. When the villagers demanded to know their names the alleged witch said they were called Silcock, Wisky, Twintail, Toby and Tegg.

A rather surprised Norfolk magistrate was told in a case in 1857 involving allegations of alleged witchcraft that a witness knew people who had seen a witch's imps. When asked by the magistrate to describe them the witness said he had been told they were like 'little things crawling about near a clock.' When pressed to describe them more clearly, the man said: 'I've heard tell they were like little mice.' (*The Times* newspaper, 27th April 1857). Mrs Smith, a witch who operated in Cambridgeshire in the early 1900s, was said to have a familiar that was described as 'a black thing'. Those who claimed to have seen it in her house reported that it was 'not exactly a dog or a rat, it looked more like a frog.' (Jennings 1905). This familiar sound like one of the strange hybrid types that was a composition of different animals or did not resemble any known animal.

During the First World War (1914–1918) a rag-and-bone man collecting household garbage in the 'witch village' of Horseheath (Cambridgeshire) was accosted by one of the local witches. She asked the man where he was going and he told her to mind her own business and not so politely go away. He had only traveled about half a mile down the lane when he heard a strange rustling sound in the hedge. The man stopped and went to investigate. He discovered the witch's imp sent to follow him and do him some harm. The man chased the creature back down the lane and it ran straight to the witch's cottage where she was standing on the doorstep. It is not recorded what the familiar looked like.

Another Cambridgeshire woman living during the First World War was regarded by the locals as the village witch. This was not unusual in rural England because, as late as the 1950s, the folklorist Theo Brown said that every village in Devon still had its own resident witch. In the Cambridgeshire case the office of village witch was a permanent one and it lasted as long as the holder of it was alive. In fact she had inherited a cage of white mice from her predecessor. These were familiars and before the present village witch died she would pass them in turn to the person who was to destined to succeed her in the role.

The most famous case of a witch and her familiar in modern times in East Anglia was that of Old Mother Redcap of Horseheath. According to Nigel Pennick, the name was a generic one given to fortune-telling women who attended fairs all over south-east England from Essex to Sussex to Cambridgeshire. It came from the distinctive headwear they always wore to show their calling. Several public houses in London also had this name. Horseheath's Old Mother Redcap was described as wearing several layers of skirts, including one tied around her waist, and a red poke bonnet whether she was outdoors or indoors. This sounds like the special costume worn by the cunning women or so-called 'white witches.'

When the witch died in 1928 *The Sunday Chronicle* newspaper reported that people in Horseheath said Old Mother Redcap had got her powers when a mysterious 'black man' (possibly a gypsy) called at her door one day. He asked her to sign her name in blood in a large black book he was carrying. He then told her she was the owner of five imps. Shortly afterwards the old woman was seen out and about in the village walking with a cat, a toad, a ferret, a rat and a mouse. One version of the story says that a witch in the village had recently died. The Man in Black was seen taking a wooden box from her house from one end of the village to the other. Evidently this was to deliver it safely to Old Mother Redcap, who had inherited the deceased witch's familiars. Yet another version says Mother Redcap inherited the spirits from her sister who lived at Castle Camps and was also a witch. Whatever the truth of the matter, the familiars were being passed from one witch to another in the old traditional way.

The imps were called Bonnie, Blue Cap, Red Cap, Jupiter and Venus. When Old Mother Redcap died it was claimed that she would still be alive if somebody had not opened the door of the hutch (small wooden house) in which she kept her imps and they had escaped. They were wrapped up in a red underskirt that was probably another significant item of clothing making up the cunning woman's costume. This story illustrates the close and symbiotic relationship between witches and their familiars.

Mark Taylor was told by a woman from Norwich in Norfolk of a story she had heard about a witch's imps. Her brother-in-law worked as a farmer and horse-breeder. Near to his farm lived an old woman who local people said had familiars. They were supposed to be called Pug, Lightfoot and Bluebell. The farmer was not a credulous or superstitious fellow and laughed when told this story. To show his contempt for the so-called witch he deliberately named three of his newborn foals after the familiars. People shook their heads and muttered that no good would come from it. Subsequently one of the horses died in an accident, the second was a 'kicker' and was useless for any work on the farm and the third went lame and had to be shot (Taylor 1929:128).

5

Wizards and Cunning Men

PROFESSOR OWEN DAVIES has claimed the term 'cunning folk' and the related individual terms 'cunning man' and 'cunning woman' are little known outside academe. However in recent years the usage of the terms has been adopted by modern practitioners following old and revived folk magic traditions. However in the past in rural England 'hundreds and thousands of people had personal experience of them...' (Davies 2003: vii). In 1625 Robert Burton claimed that 'sorcerers are too common; cunning men, wizards ['wise men'] and white witches, as they call them, in every village.' As mentioned before, every village in East Anglia was only a few miles away from a practicing cunning man.

The Essex preacher George Gifford said of the 16th century cunning man in East Anglia 'with his charm of words he can catch rats and best snakes, take away the pain of the toothache, with a pair of shears and sieve find a thief. Many other pretty knackes [tricks] he glorieth in, as if he had attained great wisdom. The cult is devilish, when anything is done the Devil worketh it, he is the instructor of the enchanter.' Just as the female witch was supposed to be in league with the Devil so in the popular belief was her male counterpart the cunning man, wizard or magician as he had also sold his soul for his magical powers.

Professor Davies has noted that the cunning man's magical activities covered all aspects of daily life. These multi-talented magical practitioners operated as diviners, astrologers, herbalists, exorcists, ghost-layers, fortune-tellers and summoners of spirits, both human and non-human. The cunning women or wise women, sometimes called 'white witches' to mark them out from those who practised malefic magic, had similar powers and talents. Thomas Heywood wrote about this in his 17th century play *The Wise Woman of Hogsden*, based on a real cunning woman he knew in London. In the play the witch says she is a fortune-teller and palmist and a diviner who can find things that are lost. She was also a healer who cured 'madd folks' and a matchmaker using her psychic abilities to bring men and women together for the purposes of love and matrimony.

One of the many widely recognized talents of the cunning folk was their ability to 'smell out witches' and because of this they often acted as unofficial witchfinders. For instance Cunning Herring of Sudbury in Suffolk both 'sniffed out witches' and practised counter-magic against those he suspected of placing spells on people. Some cunning men even made it their primary profession. George Gifford in his *Discourse of the Subtill Practices of Devilles by Witches and Sorcerers* (1587) said that if a person believed they had been 'witched' or 'overlooked' they would consult a 'wise man' for his help. He would then summon his familiar spirit to assist him in hunting down the culprit. Once the guilty party had been identified they would be handed over to the legal authorities for justice to be done. Gifford noted that at the end of the 16th century several reliable witnesses were required in a trial for murder, while only one witness, the cunning man, was needed in a witchcraft trial.

In his *Dialogue Concerning Witches and Witchcrafts* written six years later Gifford's attitude had hardened. He condemned the cunning men and 'white witches' as 'the tools of the Devil' and 'blasphemous enemies of God and mankind'. He claimed the cunning man used 'holy words' and charms to summon spirits who were really demons in disguise. They also sent innocent old women who were often regular churchgoers to their deaths. His claim was that the cunning man acted as witchfinder so he could direct attention away from his own nefarious magical activities.

Gifford said gullible people were willing to travel great distances to consult a cunning man who thy believed 'had the power.' Often the consultation came about because the client believed they had been bewitched or cursed. He cited one case where a widow went to a cunning man following the sudden death of her husband. The wizard pointedly asked her if she knew anybody who disliked him when he was alive or meant him harm. When the grieving widow named someone the man told her to gaze into a looking glass (mirror). There the woman saw the wrinkled face of an old woman wearing a pointed red cap—the traditional sign of witch. As a result of this revelation the old woman was arrested, tried for killing the woman's husband using the power of witchcraft and hanged.

In the 14th century John Holand from Woodbridge in Suffolk, a layperson who worked for the local abbey, was arrested for burglary. In court it was announced he had been arrested as the result of identification provided by a 'nigromancer,' a practitioner of the 'Black Art' or ritual magic. Holand swore under oath he was innocent and said his neighbors would testify to his good character and social standing in the community. Despite their testimonials on his behalf the court preferred to accept the evidence of the cunning man and Holand was found guilty as charged (Davies 2003:3–4).

The day-to-day professions followed by part-time cunning men, magicians and wizards were varied. Some were educated people such as schoolmasters and doctors or were connected to the medical profession in some way such as blood-letters, chemists and apothecaries. Others were shop owners, millers, shoemakers and cobblers, bodgers (workers in wood) farriers and blacksmiths, and farmers. Many could read and write and for instance the 17th century Cambridge-educated botanist Robert Turner published translations of magical tomes such as *The Notary Art of King Solomon* and Cornelius Agrippa's famous *Fourth Book of Occult Philosophy*. In 1585 a delegation from the parish of Great Bardfield in Essex petitioned to have the local schoolmaster removed from his post. He was accused of telling fortunes and performing acts of healing using charms (Sharpe 1996:69).

Many of the cunning folk were also practicing astrologers. In the 17th century a Norfolk cunning man, Christopher Hall, by trade a shoemaker, was consulted by a woman suffering from breast cancer. Hall was a 'planet-reader' or astrologer and he drew up the woman's birth chart. The cunning man told her that three women she knew in her village were responsible for her plight. They were in fact three witches and they had cursed her so that she developed her health condition and apparently in some way he divined this from his astrological calculations (Thomas 1991:757).

In 1621 an Essex astrologer, Matthew Evans, wrote to Richard Napier, who was either a magistrate or the clerk of the court, asking for the return of his magical books. These items of evidence had been mislaid when Evans was accused of practicing conjuring or the summoning of spirits. Two years later Evans was 'examined' or officially questioned by the authorities about the alleged bewitching of the Countess of Sussex, whose ancestral home was at Boreham in Essex (Macfarlane 1970:87–88).

Some cunning men and wizards were even clergymen, some actually running parishes, or were connected through their jobs with the Church. In 1528 a monk called Brother William Stapleton, from St Bennett's Abbey in Norfolk confessed to calling up 'wicked spirits' to help him find buried treasure. He said he needed money to pay for a dispensation so he could leave the Church. He had been helped in his failed endeavors at treasure-hunting by two wizards or cunning men (Davies 2003:95).

Four years later, in 1532, Thomas Sall, described as a priest based at Norwich Abbey, was criticized for neglecting his clerical duties. The reason given was that he was too busy practicing the magical arts. At the end of the same century in 1599 the Reverend John Knightley, the vicar of Gildon Morden, Cambridgeshire was acquitted on a charge of sorcery. Afterwards the cleric protested to the archdeacon at Ely Cathedral that his parishioners were still accusing him of the crime. Three years later in the *Survey of the Ministry* it was recorded that three Norfolk ministers had been reprimanded by the Church for illegally summoning spirits.

At Laindon in Essex the local minister was reputed to be a notorious practitioner of the Black Arts. The cleric hired a young village girl as his housekeeper and warned her to stay out of his study. The curious servant decided to disobey her employer. She opened the door to the room and peeped inside. Standing on the vicar's writing desk where he wrote his sermons were three small dark figures—his imps or familiars. The girl fled in terror and she never went back to the cleric's house (Maple 1965:171).

Contrary to the modern belief, the cunning folk did not usually give their services free. If no palms were crossed with silver in the traditional way, the cunning man or woman expected payment in the form of a rabbit or chicken for the pot, a jar of homemade jam or honey, a bucket of milk or half a dozen eggs. Thomas Harding in 1590 took a fee to the value of five shillings, made up of money, a side of bacon and a pigeon, for finding some lost goods. However he charged only sixpence for finding a missing child. In a rare case an Essex cunning man always refused any payment for his services. However he did admit that one of his clients voluntarily gave him a new shilling for some advice.

One Cambridgeshire cunning man said that his services were so sought after by a large number of people that he could easily earn two hundred pounds sterling a year. This was at the time when the average wage for a skilled worker was less then twenty pounds for the same period. In 1576 a Norfolk cunning man, James Stagg, asked the parents of an allegedly bewitched girl to pay a fee of six pounds and eight shillings. The parents did not have the money and the victim herself paid Stagg with five pounds from her workbox.

She told him she would pay the rest of the money when he had successfully 'unwitched' her. Unfortunately the cunning man was not happy about that arrangement. He looked around the room and saw several large seashells the parent used for decorative purposes. Stagg demanded the family turn them over as the balance of the payment. The girl's mother refused saying they were a present from her sister. The cunning man then saw some other ornaments he liked and despite the family's protests he took them instead (Davies 2003: 39 and 89).

Cunning men and wizards often employed looking glasses or mirrors to find lost property and stolen goods and to identify witches responsible for hexing their clients. In 1578 a merchant consulted a cunning man in Essex to try and find who had stolen a quantity of linen from his premises. The wizard hung an old antique mirror above a bench in his hall and told the man to look into it. After a while he saw the face of somebody he knew. The cunning man told him it was the thief who had stolen the cloth (Macfarlane 1991:125).

Another Essex cunning man, Edwin Haddesleym was accused in the reign of King James I (1603–1625) of using a 'magik glasse' or a 'conjuring glasse'. He was supposed to have used it in connection with a previous court case when he was on a charge of deer poaching. He must have been acquitted without penalty as he appeared in court again a year later. This time he was accused of bewitching two people. It is not recorded what his fate was (ibid:77).

Thomas Ady (1656) repeated a story he had been told about an Essex butcher who had lost some of his prize herd of cattle. In those days butchers kept their own livestock and slaughtered and sold them. In desperation the man contacted a well-known cunning man and was invited to his house. He was taken into a room that the wizard had set aside specially for his magical work. The butcher was told to look into a mirror and say what he saw in it. The terrified man claimed that reflected in the mirror he could see the Devil standing behind him in the shadowy corner of the room. In fact it was the cunning man's accomplice dressed in a bull's hide complete with head and horns. The 'Devil' told the butcher not to turn around. He had to go home and look east, west, north and south and he would find his missing animals. Rather naively the man returned to his farm and followed the 'satanic' instructions. After much searching for many hours high and low there was still no sign of the cattle.

He decided that the cunning man was a 'knave and a trickster' and had fooled him into paying his fee. The butcher returned to the wizard's house and asked him to conjure up the Old One again. However this time he had stationed a boy with a large and fierce mastiff dog outside the door. When the 'Devil' appeared on cue the butcher whistled and the dog was released into the room. It immediately sized the faker in the bull's costume in its jaws and would not let go. The cunning man begged the butcher to call off the dog from his assistant and offered to refund his fee (Haining 1974:191–193).

In 1584 in Cambridgeshire Edmund Mansell was accused of being a cunning man and of burning down a barn using the magical arts. In 1601 another wizard, Oliver Den, was charged with the practice of sorcery. He had given pieces of bread with 'Christian words' written on them to dogs to cure them of rabies. A witness testified that Den had also cured his hog after it was bitten by a rabid dog. The cunning man had taken an apple, cut it in half to reveal a five-pointed star formed from the seeds in its center, and written 'certain [magical] words' on it. He then fed the pig with the apple and told its owner would not recover but would also be protected in the future from the bite of mad dogs.

In 1761 a court case involving magic was reported in *The Gentleman's Magazine* published in London. An 'old sorcerer', who said he had been practicing 'The Arte' for at least thirty years, appeared in a Norwich court. He was charged under the new Witchcraft Act of 1736 with 'pretending to cure a poor woman of witchcraft'. It was not reported in the article if he was found guilty or acquitted. The report seems to have been published merely to prove to the magazine's sophisticated city readers that such superstitious beliefs still existed in rural areas and to illustrate the credulity of country people.

Nearly two hundred years ago the most famous cunning man in Ipswich in Suffolk was known as Old Winter. A farmer was regularly losing blocks of wood from his farmyard at night. He decided to call in the cunning man to solve the mystery. Old Winter lay in wait for several nights and nothing happened. Then on the next night from his hiding place he saw one of the farmer's employees enter the yard. He hoisted a block of wood on his shoulder and walked off with it. The man left the yard, entered an adjacent meadow and walked towards a stile that gave him access to the garden of his cottage. However once he had entered the field he immediately fell under a spell cast by Old Winter. He could not find the gate to his garden or leave the field. Instead he wandered aimlessly around and around in a daze carrying the heavy wood. When he was nearly collapsing from exhaustion the cunning man took pity on the thief. He whispered a few words in his ear and the spell was lifted. After the enchantment was broken the man promised never to steal anything else from his employer. This spell sounds like the condition of being 'pixy led' that in south-west England was blamed on faeries.

In the 19th century a farmer and churchwarden at Aldburgh told how he had once visited the house of a reputed wizard. He claimed that sitting on the kitchen table were the man's imps. The farmer described them as looking like 'some things' that were between a rat and a bat and they made a weird twittering sound. As soon as the cunning man realized his familiars had been seen by the visitor he commanded them to leave the room. The farmer watched in astonishment as the creatures dropped to the floor and vanished straight through the floorboards.

A Norfolk cunning man called Claypole told his many clients he had learnt his occult knowledge from reading old books on magic. He was summoned to appear at a coroner's inquest in 1880 after a woman was found dead in her bed. Around her neck was a charm supplied by the cunning man. The coroner told Claypole to pay back the money she had given him to her husband. If he refused he would be prosecuted for fraud. The cunning man was so frightened by this brush with the law that he got rid of all his magical books (Porter 1974:155).

At the end of the same century a Suffolk smallholder lost some of his plum trees to disease. Rather then blame his own neglect for not looking after the trees, he claimed a local cunning man was responsible. He said he heard the man muttering a curse on the trees as he passed by the orchard. People ridiculed the smallholder and in response he said; 'These people [cunning folk] have obtained very great power...One ought to be careful not to anger them. It is better not to speak about these people' (Gudron 1896:58).

At Wiggenhale St Germans around the same time a farmer was ru-mored to be a wizard. One day the man was watching one of his workers loading a wagon with sacks of corn to take to market. He noticed that the man had also put a bundle of the farmer's straw on the wagon. He was obviously going to sell it at the market and pocket the money for himself. When the farm worker started to set off he found the horses would not move. Whatever he did to encourage them they refused to move forward. Finally the farmer shouted at the worker: 'Take that bunch of straw off the cart boy and she will go.' The man did as he was told and the horses immediately trotted on. However, as soon as the farmer was safely out of sight, the driver went back to retrieve the straw. As soon as he put it back on the wagon the horses stood still and refused to go until he had removed it.

Jabez Few of Willingham in Cambridgeshire, who died in the 1920s, used to scare people with his familiars. They were described as looking like white rats. One day he took them into the local public house The Brewers Arms. The regulars said they could hear the creatures running up and down the stairs. However when the door was opened the cunning man's imps were nowhere to be seen. On another occasion Few put one them in the bedroom of a house of a woman called Connie Todd. Her landlord released her large ginger tomcat into the room in an attempt to get rid of the creature. There was the sound of a fierce fight in the room. When the door was opened there were lumps of ginger fur all over the floor. The terrified cat was clinging halfway up the curtains. As soon as the door opened it fled and was never seen again.

An East Anglian magical practitioner who epitomized the traditional role of a cunning man was James 'Cunning' Murrell (1780–1860). He was born in Rochford in Essex, a remote and isolated area before the coming of the railway with a reputation for witchcraft. Eric Maple has said that sickness and death were a common part of daily life to its inhabitants. Often they were blamed on the superstitious fear of the Evil Eye and the power of witches (1960).

Murrell was the seventh son of a seventh son and was therefore believed to have been born with psychic powers. He was small in height, less than five feet tall, with a countryman's ruddy complexion. His penetrating blue eyes were covered with iron-rimmed round spectacles with thick lenses, sometimes described as looking like goggles. The cunning man wore an old-fashioned and threadbare frock coat with brass buttons and a low top hat. He always carried a large gingham umbrella with thick ribs and a handle, both made of whalebone, topped with a white porcelain knob. Murrell was described as having a strange air of authority despite his diminutive size. People who met him said he was 'quick of movement, keen of eye, and sharp of face.' (Morrison 1900/1977)

Cunning Murrell.

Despite his rural upbringing, Murrell was not a country bumpkin or yokel. He was the only one in his family to be educated and was literate and well read. After leaving school he became an apprentice to a surveyor in Burnham. Later he moved to London and worked for a chemist or apothecary. There is a record in St Olav's church in the parish of Bermondsey, South London of a James Murrell marrying Elizabeth Frances Button on August 12th 1812. In the same year Murrell returned to Rochford and set up a business as a shoemaker and cobbler. He fathered twenty children and when he was widowed in 1839 became a professional cunning man based in the village of Hadleigh.

It was rumored that while he was living in London Cunning Murrell may have become a student of the famous occultist Francis Barrett, the author of the influential magical grimoire *The Magus* (1801). When he moved back to Essex and became a cunning man Murrell's fame quickly spread. When the cunning man died a vast quantity of letters was found in a chest in his cottage. They came from people all over Essex and Suffolk and as far away as Kent and London. From this correspondence it was clear that wealthy women in the capital city consulted Murrell. They had evidently heard about his powers from the Essex girls they employed as maids and kitchen staff.

Cunning Murrell was widely respected because of his natural gift of the Second Sight, his abilities as an astrologer and predictor of the future, and his wide botanical knowledge enabling him to make and prescribe herbal medicines. Apparently he grew his own herbs in his cottage garden. He also claimed to be able to exorcise ghosts, banish evil spirits, restore lost property and, most importantly, lift the curses placed by so-called 'black witches'. He also worked extensively as a healer treating both humans and animals using the laying-on of hands, incantations, charms and protective amulets. Murrell owned a crystal ball and a 'magick mirror' for scrying and a special telescope that he claimed could see through walls. He also had a copper charm that he claimed told him if a person was lying or not.

The wizard lived in a small clapboard, two-storey cottage in a row of a dozen others situated in a narrow lane off Hadleigh High Street near the parish church. The rooms in the cottage were packed with Murrell's extensive collection of occult books and astrological almanacs. One of the books frequently consulted by Murrell consisted of fifty handwritten pages and was entitled the *Book of Magic and Conjurations*. At least some of its pages contained material taken from Barrett's *The Magus* so clearly Murrell had read it. From the low rafters of the front room of the cottage hung bunches of drying herbs to be used in remedies. In one corner was an elaborately carved 18th century wooden chest, now owned by the museum in Southend-on-Sea, in which he kept magical manuscripts and the correspondence from his clients. On the table were a human skull and a ritual knife. A large brass telescope, representing his history in astronomy, stood next to the hearth by an old high backed chair in which Murrell sat when receiving visitors.

When somebody called on the cunning man they were asked to state their reason for visiting him. He also had a network of local informants who provided him with intelligence and relied on gossip about local affairs. Depending on the information he had Murrell would decide on a suitable course of action and if either 'low' or 'high' magic was required. Material help was provided by the making of an herbal remedy, a charm written on parchment or an amulet or talisman. If 'high' magic was needed then the wizard would do a ritual to summon 'good angels' to combat the powers of darkness. He charged a fee between sixpence and a shilling or half a crown (two shillings and sixpence) if he had to conjure up spirits.

When tracing stolen or lost goods Murrell brought his 'magick mirror' into play. In the 1950s Eric Maple was told about this object by an elderly inhabitant in Hadleigh whose father had consulted the cunning man when he was a young boy. He had lost some money from a drawer and asked Murrell if he could find it. The cunning man told the boy to look into his mirror. At first he saw nothing but swirling mist and then it cleared and he saw his own mother in the glass. Murrell said she had only borrowed the money and would pay it back, and that in fact came to pass.

When Cunning Murrell battled with practitioners of malefic magic he used the traditional method of a 'witch bottle.' These were filled with some of the urine from the victim of bewitchment and their nail clippings, a few drops of blood, a lock of hair and some bent pins and nails. The bottle was then sealed with wax and a cork and placed on an open fire. The contents were boiled until the bottle grew so hot from the steam inside that it exploded. This was supposed to release the spell, destroy the witch's power over the victim and force them to reveal themselves. Considering the bottle's contents this was quite a risky and dangerous procedure.

The witch bottles used by Murrell were specially made for him from iron by the village blacksmith, Stephen Choppen. In the 1890s the smith told the novelist Arthur Morrison when he visited Hadleigh that he had problems making the first magical vessel for the cunning man. He could not understand why and the problem was only solved when Murrell visited the smithy and blew on the flames of the forge. The blacksmith was then able to complete the task successfully (Morrison 1900).

In the 1850s a young woman called Sarah Mott went into a barn and found an old gypsy woman sleeping rough. She chased her out and the old woman muttered under her breath: 'You'll be sorry for this my girl.' Shortly afterwards Mott began having extreme fits. She ran around on all fours mewing like a cat and barking like a dog. Witnesses even claimed she climbed up the walls and walked about on the ceiling like a fly. Her parents were convinced the girl was demonically possessed and they called in Cunning Murrell. He confirmed their suspicions and suggested a witch bottle was prepared containing a small amount of the girl's urine and blood together with a few pins and 'magical' herbs. The vessel was placed on the kitchen fire and heated up. The room was in darkness apart from the light from the flames and the door had been locked.

Then the watchers heard footsteps shuffling up to the door. A pitiful female voice cried out; 'For God's sake stop! You are killing me!' At that very moment the bottle exploded and the crying of the voice outside suddenly ceased. Sarah Mott immediately recovered and next day it was said the badly burned body of the old gypsy woman was found outside a local public house. The witch bottle had certainly worked its magic and the cunning man had triumphed again.

In 1858, two years before Cunning Murrell's death, *The Essex Standard* reported that 'in this enlightened age instances of the grossest superstition [are] prevailing in our rural parishes of this county.' The newspaper said that at East Thorpe in Essex a young woman called Emma Brazier from a local farming family had been using 'the most violent, abusive and filthy language' against her neighbor Mrs Mole, who she had accused of bewitching her. The Brazier family complained that the woman had cast spells on their livestock, in one case actually making a pig climb an apple tree and eat all the fruit on it. The family decided to bring in a cunning man to deal with the problem.

They consulted one who was popularly known as the 'Wizard of the North', but he proved to be no match for Mrs Mole's powers and was defeated. Undeterred, the Braziers then contacted Cunning Murrell from Hadleigh because they had heard of his great reputation for banishing curses and ill-wishing. He sent the family through the post a bottle of herbal medication for the daughter to calm her down and enclosed a bill for hree shillings. Murrell also promised that he would come to the village as soon as possible to confront the alleged witch and warn her off.

In the meantime the local vicar, who had been away from the parish on church business while this was going on, returned. He was horrified to find what he regarded as a 'a gross outbreak of ignorance and superstition' among his flock. He visited the allegedly bewitched girl and, after hearing the story and examining her, the minister concluded she was insane. In his opinion for her own safety and that or her family she should be locked up in a lunatic asylum. On his advice Emma Brazier was seen by a doctor who confirmed the clergyman's diagnosis and she was committed to the local workhouse. The vicar also contacted the local magistrate and obtained a promise that the police would keep a watchful eye on the neighborhood. This was so the suspected witch would not come to any harm from vigilantes.

When Cunning Murrell arrived in the village his presence caused quite a stir. He immediately went to Mrs Mole's cottage to see the alleged witch. As soon as news of the cunning man's arrival spread a noisy crowd of about a hundred people gathered from far and wide. This gathering, said the newspaper, was characterized by its 'drunkenness and riotous conduct.' To protect Mrs Mole from the violence of the mob the vicar was forced to stand guard at the front door of her cottage. All this took place within sight of the parish constable's house. However, having seen the size and ugly mood of the mob, he decided to stay safely indoors. Eventually police officers from outside the village arrived and dispersed the angry crowd with their truncheons or batons.

The final outcome of this nasty incident was that Emma Brazier was released from her confinement. However she then had to appear before the magistrate charged with threatening Mrs Mole's life. She was bound over to keep the peace and that seems to have been the end of the affair. Cunning Murrell appears to have escaped without any official censure for his role in the sorry business and two years later he was dead.

Public opinion about James Murrell was divided and ambiguous. The local vicar, the Reverend Thomas Espin, had been a professor of theology at Queens College in Birmingham. He had spent many hours discussing religion with the cunning man and always lost the argument. In the end the minister admitted Murrell knew the Bible better than he did. Espin said that he could not make up his mind about him. He was either a good man or a very bad man and the vicar had not decided which was true. The gentry regarded Murrell as a 'quack doctor' and a charlatan, while the lower class held him in high regard, although their respect was tinged with fear of his powers.

The cunning man claimed to be the 'Devil's master' and that is why he had the power to exorcise demons and combat the spells and curses of witches. Others said it was because he was secretly in league with Old Nick and had sold his soul for his powers. Murrell was also known as a 'master of witches' because he allegedly had the power to control the sisterhood and submit them to his will. He was supposed to have once engaged in a magical duel with one of the famous witches of Canewdon to demonstrate the power of his 'white magic' over her 'black magic.' He won by telling her 'I command you to die' and she allegedly fell to the ground dead. Such fantastic stories were often told about the cunning man to illustrate his powers over the local witches.

Local gossip also associated Cunning Murrell with the criminal activities of smuggling gangs. On clear nights he used to leave his cottage with his umbrella over his arm and carrying his telescope and a basket over his arm. He claimed he went out into the countryside to collect plants from the hedgerows for his remedies or to 'star gaze.' He was often spotted on these nocturnal trips by the smugglers and the Revenue men who were hunting for them. One dark moonless night the landlord of a local inn who was secretly involved in the contraband trade saw strange lights on a hill and thought it was the Revenue. He went to investigate and found Cunning Murrell standing on the hill surrounded by dancing globes of blue light, which the terrified man interpreted as spirits.

After Cunning Murrell's death several smugglers claimed to have seen his ghost. On one occasion it was said that a local witch who had been friendly with the cunning man appeared in the shape of an unusually large badger near his grave in Hadleigh churchyard. In fact when Murrell had been alive the smugglers had been attacked by such a creature when they tried to approach the cunning man on the downs at night. Murrell was also seen simultaneously sitting in his chair by the hearth in his cottage smoking his long stemmed clay pipe and standing out on the downs gazing up at the sky. To placate the wizard so he did not interfere too much in their activities the smugglers often left a barrel of French brandy outside his front door.

In late 1860 at the age of eighty James Murrell was taken ill. He asked his son to bring him paper and pen. He used them to make astrological calculations and predicted correctly he would die on December 16th. As he lay dying he was visited by the then vicar, the delightfully named Reverend John Godson, seeking to convert him to Christianity on his deathbed. Murrell however refused to have anything to do with the Church. He defended his use of magical powers and the good work he had done with them with the last gasp of his breath. Murrell was interred in an unmarked gave in the churchyard of Hadleigh's parish church near his cottage with his wife and most of his children buried nearby. His death certificate said 'James Murrell: Profession Quack Doctor: Natural Causes'. Not surprisingly a rival wizard from Rayleigh claimed that he had 'unnaturally done Murrell' using one of the cunning man's own trademark witch bottles. Such claims were not unusual and are still made today when a well-known magical practitioner or witch dies.

Murrell's last wish was that he could pass on his virtue or 'power' before he passed over to the spirit world. This was very similar to the 'passing on of power or virtue and familiar spirits by witches. Unfortunately his only surviving son, Edward, nicknamed 'Buck', (1824–1903), was illiterate and quite unworthy to don his father's mantle. However he was quite skilled at wart-charming and after his father's death he did make a futile attempt to follow in his footsteps with an unfortunate result.

Buck Murrell found the last witch bottle made by the blacksmith for his father. A man who suspected that he was bewitched consulted the cunning man's son thinking he had inherited his father's powers. Buck placed the vessel on the fire and the two men sat down on either side of the hearth and waited. The bottle boiled and boiled and nothing happened. The client became impatient and said; 'I don't believe this witch bottle's a good 'un.' No sooner had the fateful words left his mouth then the bottle finally burst. The explosion not only knocked the two men out of their chairs, it also destroyed the chimneypiece, grate and hearth and blew a large hole in the wall of the cottage. That was the last time a frightened and chastised Buck Murrell attempted any form of magical practice (Morrison 1900).

After Cunning Murrell's death his whalebone umbrella was given to the local undertaker who buried him. The chest that contained his magical books was passed to a woman he knew in Southend-on-Sea who later donated it to the local museum. Unfortunately although they still own it the object is not on public display. The telescope was sold by Buck Murrell for half a guinea (ten shillings and sixpence) to a local resident. A little while later its new owner was found dead. He had a half guinea coin lodged in his throat that had choked him. A local historian Phillip Benton, author of *A History of the Rochford Hundreds*, acquired two human skulls the cunning man had owned and used in his magical rituals.

Murrell's landlord buried all his magical books and papers in the garden of the cottage believing he had carried a public service so they did not fall into the wrong hands. However Buck Murrell found out and secretly dug them up. When the novelist Arthur Morrison visited Hadleigh in the 1890s the cunning man's son showed him the books and many of the letters from enquirers. The volumes included academic works on astronomy, medicine and botany, an original copy of Nicholas Culpeper's famous herbal published in 1649, and astrological almanacs. There were also a number of handwritten books containing information on angelic magic, the conjuration of spirits, occult correspondences, charms, the preparation of amulets and talismans, the geomantic art of divination and some Cabbalistic sigils. These were the stock-in-trade of all the cunning men who could read and write.

Eric Maple claimed these books survived as late as 1956 when their owner decided they were worthless and destroyed them. Only one is supposed to have survived and was possibly owned by a local doctor. It contained astrological data, some material by the 17th century wizard Neoboad in his own handwriting and a birth chart and horoscope of Queen Victoria (reigned 1837–1901) drawn up by Murrell himself. In 1993 the then owner of the book offered it to the library of the Folklore Society in London. For some reason the offer was not taken up. The present whereabouts of the book are not known. It can only be hoped that the book has somehow passed into the hands of another Essex cunning person or magical practitioner or will do so in the future.

Although Buck Murrell did not take on his father's work because of the unfortunate accident with the witch bottle, there have been hints that others carried on the tradition. Cunning Murrell referred to the belief that there will always be nine witches in Canewdon, one in Leigh-on-Sea and three in Hadleigh. In an article 'The Story of the Essex Witches' in his magazine *Earthquest News* (Vol 3, Issue 4, Winter 2000) and 'Essex Witchcraft Investigated' in this writer's magazine *The Cauldron* (No 99, February 2001) psychic questor and bestselling author Andrew Collins wrote about this intriguing comment by Murrell.

Collins believes that the reference to the three witches in Hadleigh was in fact to three local witch families. They have, he claims, passed on knowledge and written material from one generation to another down the distaff or female line since the 19th century and before. He further claims to know one of the descendants of the three witches, a young woman who is next in line after her grandmother and mother. At the appointed time she will receive the passing on of 'the book' dating from the time of Cunning Murrell. She must then move within a league (three miles) of St James' church in Hadleigh. 'The book' is a handwritten manuscript containing herbal lore, magical seals and occult correspondences. The handing down of such written materials is a well-known means of 'passing the power' in traditional witchcraft circles, past and present.

One of James Murrell's daughters, Hannah, married a man from Canewdon in 1829 and went to live in the village. It is probable that her father went to visit them on several occasions. In fact people said that often Murrell would arrive in the village just after dark and leave again at dawn. He therefore would likely have met his contemporary the local village cunning man and wizard, Old George Pickingill (1816–1909). It has even been speculated that another of Murrell's daughters, Ann Pett, may have married into the extended Pickingill family (James 1982). It is also claimed that the villagers in Canewdon petitioned the vicar to ask him to invite Cunning Murrell to 'whistle up the witches' and expose them. The vicar, the Reverend Atkinson, was supposed to have blocked the move because his wife was allegedly a member of the local coven.

George Pickingill or Pickingale or Pettingale, the surname is spelt several different ways in official documents and records, was born in Hockley in Essex in 1816—a year after the Battle of Waterloo when the British and their Prussian allies defeated Napoleon Bonaparte. Old George's father, Charles Pickingill (1790–1867) was married to a Susannah or Hannah Cudmore. He was an agricultural laborer and variously lived in Canewdon, Hockley and Street. Old George himself also moved about and lived in Hockley, Eastwood and Canewdon in Essex and briefly Gravesend in Kent, where it is possible he had Romany relatives. It has been alleged that they visited him in the village of Canewdon when he later lived there and performed rituals led by Pickingill in the graveyard of the village church, until disturbed by the vicar (Lefurbe 1970:55).

Old George had two daughters and two sons. One of his sons, also called George, served time in Chelmsford Prison in 1891 and died in 1903. George Pickingill's sister Catherine married a farmer called Cocks (later changed to Cox) from Hockley and they immigrated to Canada in

FACING: Old George Pickingill of Canwedon.

Dickingale 109 Years old

1874. Her sister Martha Smith had emigrated the year before. The family lived in Fitzroy near Ontario and Manitoba and were farmers (pers. com Kimberli Shepstone, 24th October 2010). Pickingill's grandson was in the Coldstream Guards in the First World War and the grandson of his daughter Martha was also killed in action in the trenches. Recently the writer was contacted by one of Pickingill's relatives in Canada. She had read about his connection with witchcraft while researching her family history on the Internet. This had surprised her and she wanted to know more about her English ancestor's activities as a cunning man. Evidently the art of witchcraft had not been passed down in her part of the family.

The Pickingill family had long historical connections with the 'witch village' of Canewdon. There is a parish record of a payment made to a Thomas Pickingale in October 1706 of two shillings and sixpence for 'laying out the dead'. He was also paid for washing and mending a surplice. Another Thomas Pickingale was the church sexton and gravedigger until his death in 1804. In 1791 he was paid three shillings and four pence for the burial of Sarah Rogers. Mrs Pickingale, presumably his wife, was paid 'three shillings and tuppence' in April 1791 for laying out a dead man, shaving him and making his shroud. Considering the witchcraft interests of their 19th century descendant this family connection to the dead and churchyards is interesting.

The Pickingill or Pickingale family was well documented in parish records in East Anglia, and also in local court records. Several of Old George's siblings and relatives were jailed for petty crimes like stealing vegetables from their neighbors' gardens. This was not that unusual as most ordinary country people of the time lived in conditions of harsh poverty that forced them to carry out minor criminal acts. In the 1850s *The Examiner* newspaper published in London carried a report that a man called Pettingale had been shot dead during the annual fair in Castle Rising. The Pickingills were spread widely all over the East Anglia but mostly lived in Essex and Norfolk. The cunning man George Pickingill of Canewdon also had relatives who lived at Castle Rising in Norfolk. In 1963 this ancient village was the scene of an outbreak of traditional witchcraft involving poppets or wax images fixed to the castle door. Others were found in ruined churches in the area.

When he moved to Canewdon and worked as a farm laborer Old George Pickingill lived in a cottage near the village well in the High Street. He was well known locally as the 'Wise Man of Canewdon' and was widely respected and feared in equal measure by the villagers. Pickingill was described as 'a gaunt ragged creature, dirty, unkempt and fierce, with piercing eyes which terrified all who saw him'. He had long uncut fingernails and carried his money around in a makeshift purse made from sacking (Maple 1960 and 1962:185). Old George wore a long black coat and always carried a distinctive blackthorn walking stick that was said to be his 'blasting rod'. The cunning man used it to 'blast' or paralyse people who crossed him. At harvest time Pickingill was supposed to have gone into the fields and threatened to bewitch the farm machinery. The farmers bribed him with jugs of beer to stay away and he often ended the day drunk in a hedge.

In common with his contemporary Cunning James Murrell, Pickingill was reputed to be a 'master of witches.' It was said he could summon the seven or nine witches who allegedly lived in Canewdon by blowing a silver whistle. When this writer visited the village in the 1970s he met 'Granny' Lillian Garner (1890–1982), who was born Lillian Higby in India, where her father was a British Army officer. Her family was of Dutch origin and had come to East Anglia when the Hollanders used their expertise to help drain the fens. Lillian had traveled widely around the world due to her marriage to a lieutenant in the Royal Navy.

Granny Garner was well known in the village as a 'white witch' even though her family had lived in Vicarage Cottage and worked for the church for many years. The Higbys moved into the cottage after it ceased to be the temporary village school and they also ran a tearoom. Lillian was consulted for healing and when people believed they had been bewitched. She advised them to put scissors or a pair of sewing shears under the doormat 'to keep them witches out.' She is also said to have followed in Cunning Murrell's footsteps by preparing witch bottles to identify practitioners of malefic magic and lift their curses. Lillian was also very psychic as she had seen many of the ghosts that are supposed to haunt Canewdon. She was Eric Maple's chief informant when he visited the village in 1959 researching the local witchcraft legends. He also invited the older people to either the parish hall or the school to talk about their reminiscences of the local witches (pers.comm, Sibyl Webster, February 10th 2008).

Lillian had known Old George Pickingill when she was a child living in the village. She remembered him as an eccentric character and 'the oldest man in England' who was photographed next to the first car seen in Canewdon. This event was reported in a London newspaper and the *Southend Standard and Essex Weekly Advertiser* on September 27th 1908, shortly before he died. Lillian Garner said that Pickingill was the 'witch master' of a coven in Canewdon and that her mother told her she belonged to it. As a typical cunning man Old George also cured minor ailments and did healing such as stopping the flow of blood when local farm workers cut themselves. He also found lost property and stolen goods and by magical means identified the thieves. Lillian Garner also claimed he was visited by 'people from far away' who came to consult him on occult matters. She knew nothing about modern witchcraft and had not read any magazines or books on the subject except the copy of Eric Maple's book that he sent her when it was published.

Old George Pickingill died on April 2nd 1909, aged 93. His death was reported in obituaries in the local newspaper *The Southend Observer* and in *Lloyd's Weekly News* (April 11th 1909) in London, although they did not mention his role as a cunning man. The obituaries incorrectly claimed that he was 106 years old when he died. The *Lloyd's Weekly News* said that one of their reporters visited Canewdon in 1908 to interview the 'oldest man in England' who was known to villagers as 'Old Daddy.' He falsely told the journalist he remembered the news of victory in the Battle of Waterloo arriving in the village. Evidently Pickingill was a person who was economical with the truth.

It is claimed that before he died Old George said that he would make a final demonstration of his magical powers at his funeral. As the hearse arrived at the church gate the horses are supposed to have stepped out of the shafts and trotted away. Strange events reported at the burial of reputed witches were not unusual. At Rockland in Norfolk a storm arose when a witch was interred. As the time of the funeral grew closer the wind and rain increased in intensity with loud claps of thunder and flashes of lightning. In fact as the bearers carried the coffin into the churchyard the wind was so strong that they found it difficult to stay upright. However as the witch's coffin was lowered into the ground the storm stopped just as suddenly as it had began (Porter 1974:149)

6

Toad, Horse and Hare Magic

IN EAST ANGLIA, as elsewhere, one of the favorite familiars of witches and wizards were toads. This has a historical provenance as in the 16th century Jeanette d' Abadie, a witch from the Pyrenees mountain range between France and Spain, confessed to having toads as familiars. The court was told she had baptized the amphibians with names and dressed them up in black and scarlet velvet coats she had made with bells on the sleeves. For this blatant act of blasphemy she was burnt at the stake.

The important role of toads as witches' familiars is reflected in the folklore that connects them with the supernatural and witchcraft. In fact they are mentioned in William Shakespeare's Scottish play as being used by the three witches on the blasted heath:

> Round about the cauldron go;
> In the poison'd entrails throw
> Toad that under cold stone
> Days and nights has thirty-one
> Swelt' red venom sleeping got
> Be thou first i' th'charmed pot.
> *Macbeth*, Act 4, Scene 1

The reference in the above charm to 'poison'd entrails' and 'red venom' refers to the popular belief that toads were poisonous or exuded poison. In fact the skins and glands of some toads do excrete the toxin *bufotenin*, commonly known as 'toad's milk' that can affect the human nervous system. The effects of these secretions are similar to those of the common foxglove plant, from which is derived the modern drug digitalis. At high dosage they can cause heart failure in both humans and animals. Digitalis was actually discovered by a Shropshire doctor who was told about the effects of foxglove by a local wise woman. In some countries medicines are made from small amounts of toad venom and are used for a wide range of common complaints.

The breath of a toad was also considered as poisonous as its skin and highly dangerous. It was also believed that if a toad looked at you for too long you would develop fits. These included muscular spasms, convulsions and paralysis of the limbs. French witches used toads in a recipe for a potion for flying to the Sabbat. They stole a consecrated host from a church and fed it the toads. The animals were then killed and their bodies cremated. The ashes were mixed with powdered human bone and blood and narcotic herbs to create a potion or ointment. A mixture of sow thistle sap and toad spittle was supposed to make a witch invisible when she traveled by normal means to the Sabbat.

In East Anglia there was a form of cursing called 'tudding', meaning bewitching, after the country nickname 'tuddy' for a toad. There was also the expression 'putting the toad' on referring to the placing of a curse using the animal. This involved burying a toad on a path near the victim's house that they walked along every day. It was said that the curse could be lifted by catching another toad and rather cruelly boiling it in hot water in a saucepan. It was claimed that this act of sympathetic magic would cause agony to the witch who had placed the curse and negate their power over the victim. However toads could also be used for healing illnesses and diseases. The body of one worn in a velvet or muslin bag around the neck warded off the malefic power of 'owl blinking' or the Evil Eye.

At Dereham in Suffolk in the 1870s a case of 'tudding' actually resulted in a court case. A man called William Bulwer was charged with assaulting a 16-year-old girl because he believed her mother was a witch and had 'put the toad on him.' Apparently Bulwer was having trouble sleeping and one night got up and went out into the garden. There he found a 'walking toad' concealed under a clod of earth that had been dug up with a three-pronged fork by the 'old witch.' After taking the animal indoors to show to his mother he threw the toad out of this bedroom window. The next day he saw the alleged witch's daughter in the street and attacked her. The magistrate was unconvinced by his defense and

Bulwer was fined a shilling for the assault and ordered to pay twelve shillings and sixpence in court costs (*The Folklore Record* 1879).

In 1329 an Italian monk, Peter Recordi, was sentenced to death for practicing sorcery. The Inquisition said he had made images using wax mixed with toad's blood and spittle. He had consecrated these wax images to his master the Devil before planting them secretly in the house of a woman he knew. It was claimed that this was a form of amatory magic to make her have sex with the licentious monk. The court records do not say if he was successful or not (Russell 1972:186). Priests, monks and even popes were often accused of practicing the magical arts. One famous grimoire was even named after a pope called Honorius and he also gave his name to a magical alphabet used by witches and cunning folk.

Some toads were believed by gullible people to have a precious stone embedded in their foreheads. It was supposed to be a powerful talisman that produced 'perfect happiness' in its owner and alchemists believed it was the famed Philosopher's Stone that transformed lead into gold. In fact this alchemical process known as the Great Work was about the transformation of the material to the spiritual. The legendary toad stone could also be used to detect poison as it became hot and glowed in its vicinity. One dropped into a goblet of wine or a jug of ale would show if it had been tampered with or poisoned had been added. Sometimes the toad stone was set into a ring for this purpose. One example from the 14th century was found to contain only the fossil of an ancient fish.

In eastern England as well as being witches' familiars the toad was used in another form of magic or sorcery known as the 'Waters of the Moon'. This was the obtaining of the 'toad bone amulet' by means of performing the 'toad bone rite' and its use for magical purposes. Frogs were also used for the ritual. The earliest reference to this amulet can be dated back to Roman times. Pliny the Elder in his *Historia Naturalis* published in 79 CE mentioned placing a toad in an earthenware pot and burying it alive to stop storms. He also referred to obtaining a toad bone by allowing ants to eat the amphibian's flesh away. The skeleton was then placed in running water and when it broke up a bone from the right side was taken for magical use. Reginald Scot in his book *Discoverie of Witchcraft* (1584) described an identical ritual. The bone that did not sink in the water and floated was selected and wrapped in a white linen cloth. It could then be used for love magic. A toad bone placed in wine also acted as an aphrodisiac. Possession of the toad bone gave its owner the power over horses, pigs, cattle and women and was also used for wart charming. To get rid of warts the bone was rubbed on the infected area of skin. More fantastically possession of a toad bone was supposed make its owner invisible, see in the dark, unlock doors and escape detection if they committed a crime.

The modern folklorist George Ewart Evans said that the person who performed this ritual in East Anglia, the Toadman, was regarded as a male witch who had sold his soul to the Devil. Sometimes the toad bone was explicitly called the 'witch bone.' Ewart Evans described the method of getting the toad or frog bone amulet as described to him by a Norfolk man, Albert Love, who was born in 1886. Love called the actual toad bone ritual 'The Water of the Moon' and told Evans that a 'walking toad' or natterjack toad was the best. These had to be taken from a special place as they were collected from Fritton near Great Yarmouth. The magical procedure was to kill the toad and hang it on a whitethorn branch. It was left for 24 hours to dry out and then buried in an ant hill.

The toad was kept in the ant hill for a lunar month (28 days) from one new or full moon to the next. The cleaned skeleton of the toad was then taken to a stream at the magically liminal time of midnight and when the moon's disc or crescent could be seen in the sky. This was known as 'going to the river.' The bones were thrown into the running water and the one that left the rest and floated upstream was kept. Usually this was the crotch bone or the forked pelvic bone known as the illium. This bone could then be used for magical purposes.

If the person performing the ritual was distracted and took their eyes off the floating bones the whole procedure would be null and void. They also had to be careful not to lose their focus due to noises such as the wind in the trees or even more dramatic sounds like thunder, buildings collapsing or the engine of a steam traction engine or in modern times a tractor. Albert Love said he had failed when doing the ritual for a third time when he heard a loud crackling noise. He took his eyes off the bones and when he retrieved the special one it had no magical power. Love claimed the sound was connected with the toad bone ritual being 'the Devil's work.'

East Anglian resident E. G. Bates related the story of a man he was told about who decided to do the toad bone ritual. He was about to throw the skeletal remains into a stream when his friends who were watching from a distance saw him run away without doing it. When they caught up with the fleeing man and asked him what was wrong he said he had become frightened by the thunder and lightning. His friends were puzzled as they had heard nothing and the night sky was totally cloudless (1939:70).

Once the toad-bone amulet had been acquired the Toadman either carried it in his pocket or wallet or he took it home and baked it in an oven. It was then reduced to powder and stored in a small tin, snuff box, tobacco pouch or bottle. Mixed with one of the special 'jading' or 'drawing' oils used to calm horses a small quantity of this powdered bone was place on the finger. It was then rubbed on the horse's nose, tongue and chest. Love said from then on '...he's your servant; you can do what you like with him' Alternatively the toad bone could be rubbed directly on to the horse's skin (Evans 1974:217–219).

A similar account of the toad bone ritual was given in the 1930s in a book edited by Lilias Rider Haggard, the grandson of the Victorian adventure writer H. Rider Haggard, who lived in Norfolk and was the author of *King Solomon's Mines*. The book was called *I Walked By Night: Being the Life & History of the King of the Norfolk Poachers* and it was reprinted by The Boydell Press in 1974. The poacher of the title was born in a small Norfolk village around 1860 and said his 'old granny' was a wise woman visited by people seeking cures. She was the village midwife and layer out of the dead and also told fortunes using tea leaves in a cup. She taught her grandson her charms, which she claimed where at least two hundred years old.

One of these charms was the making of a toad bone amulet. The witch-granny said that a toad with a yellow ring around its neck had to be caught. The toad was then placed in a perforated box so it could still breathe and buried alive in an ant hill. Once it had died and all the flesh had decomposed or been eaten by the ants the skeleton was removed from the box. It was then taken to a stream at midnight on St Agnes Eve (April 25th) and thrown into the running water. One of the bones would sink and that was the special one as it would enable its owner to control both animals and humans, especially women but also men. It also granted the power from the Devil to practice witchcraft.

The modern Essex cunning man and magician the late Andrew D. Chumbley (1967–2004), who performed the toad bone rite himself, mentioned correspondence he had with the traditional witch Evan John Jones in 1999. Jones told him about a farmer he knew where he lived in Sussex who had performed the toad bone ritual to actually become a witch. The man used the toad bone amulet in his daily farm work, but also in his role as the leader of a group practicing traditional witchcraft (Chumbley 2011).

A story from East Anglia about the toad bone rite also suggests that it sometimes represented one of the forms of entry into the witch-cult. After the special bone had been taken from the water by the Toadman, who as mentioned earlier was popularly regarded as a warlock or male witch, he took it to a stable for three consecutive nights, probably the three nights of the full moon. On the third visit the Devil would materialize and try to wrest the bone from its owner. If this attempt was successfully resisted then the Old One would draw some blood from him and this action would make the bone's owner a fully fledged and initiated Toadman.

Ownership of the toad bone amulet sometimes had unfortunate consequences. There are stories of people suffering misfortune or even going insane after performing the rite. In 1950 a woman from Camberton in Cambridgeshire revealed that her grandfather had confessed shortly before he died that he was a Toadman. He said that following the ritual he had only exercised his newly gained power over horses just two or three times. After that he stopped doing it as he was frightened of the terrible consequences that might follow.

One Toadman was an old farmer who used to walk back from the pub in the dark even if he was very drunk. Sometimes he was accompanied back to the farmhouse by his housekeeper who always remained sober. Often the man would look back over his shoulder and claim he was being followed by the Devil. This feeling of supernatural dread was apparently connected with the toad bone rite he had carried out. The farmer asked his companion if she could see anybody. She responded by saying there was nobody lurking in the darkness and he was just 'An old fool!' (Porter 1974:57).

Witches were supposed to be able to stop horses and horse-drawn and other wheeled vehicles and prevent them from moving. When automobiles started appearing on the roads at the beginning of the 20th century this magical practice was transferred to them as well. This was also a form of magic practised by the Toadmen using the power of the toad bone. In 1927 a Cambridgeshire man from Wisbech borrowed two horses from a local farmer. He said he needed to go to the railway station and collect a wagon of wood to make a new pigsty. When he took the animals from the stable the head horseman was not there. However as he collected the wagon the man rode by on his bicycle and asked what was going on and how he acquired his employer's horses.

On receiving the explanation the horseman casually remarked that the man would not be able to move the wagon and rode off. This prophetic remark came true as no matter what he did the vehicle would not move an inch. When the farmer heard what had happened he told the man to ask the head horseman to bring three horses to pull the wagon. This was done and only one of the new horses was required to move the wagon and its load of wood. Afterwards the farmer explained to the man that his employee had been annoyed as he was not consulted about borrowing the horses. He was a Toadman and in his anger had put a spell on the wagon so that its wheels would not move until he released it (Porter 1974: 58).

Toadmen did not only control and have mastery over horses and other animals. They were also supposed to gain the ability to see in the dark and also see the wind. An additional power provided by the ownership of the toad bone charm was the malefic one of the Evil Eye. Alternatively this could be gained by catching nine toads, tying them together with a piece of twine or string and burying them alive. This gave the witch the power to 'owl blast' or 'overlook' people, psychically binding them so they could not move or cause physical injury and death (Pennick 1995:61). George Ewart Evans discovered that in one Suffolk village a man was renowned for charming warts. People said he had acquired the healing power after performing the rite with a frog bone and selling his soul to the Devil. Although many villages in eastern England had their resident charmer, Evans says this was the first time he had heard of the this magical rite being associated with them (1975:247).

Although the toad bone rite was usually a male preserve, as was seen from the story of the Norfolk poacher's grandmother it could also be performed by women. One famous example was Tilly Baldrey from Huntingtoft in Norfolk. She caught and killed a natterjack toad and ignoring any hygiene concerns kept it 'in her bosom' (under her blouse close to her breasts) until it rotted away. Then she took the bones to running water at midnight on the full moon. The Devil was supposed to have appeared and to have 'dragged her over the water'. It was said that this is the way Baldrey got her power to 'dew all minder of badness to people and her power over them.' (Ibid:150).

When Baldrey's husband ran off with another younger woman called Neoma Cason the Toadwoman was determined to have her revenge.

First of all she cast a charm on her errant husband. He was forced to walk sixteen miles backwards to their former marital home from where his new lover lived. The witch then managed to obtain a lock of Cason's hair and burnt it in a candle flame. As a result the adulterous woman became ill and began to waste away. Cason went to a wizard who correctly identified Toadwoman as the source of her sickness. He told her that if she wanted to be free from her power she must get hold of some of the ashes from the Toadwoman's burnt hair. Unfortunately Neoma Cason was too ill and could not manage it as the cunning man had instructed and she died. Tilly Baldry hypocritically attended the funeral and in a last mocking gesture threw ashes from Cason's own burnt hair that she had acquired into the open grave.

Once it was said that despite all her powers the Toadwoman was outwitted by a fellow practitioner of the magical arts. Baldry and a fellow witch, Sybil Isbill, had both fallen out with a local farmer because he had stopped supplying them with milk. In revenge the two women bewitched the farmer's churns so the butter he was making went sour. Mysteriously all his cows were also released from their pasture one night. The next morning they were found roaming all over the countryside and it took the man all day to round them up.

The farmer asked for the advice of a 'wise man' from Norwich who told him to lock and bar all the doors and windows to the cow shed and the dairy. He was also to tie ropes around the bewitched churns. If he did this the two witches would be forced against their will to come to the farm and attempt access. The farmer said that if they did he would shoot them both dead. The cunning man told him to do nothing and not even talk to them. It came to pass that Baldry and Isbill 'ratticked at the doors, they hallered and they blarred until they were right dumb' (lost their voices). The farmer would not let them in or speak to them and that broke the spell so the butter was never spoiled again by the two witches (ibid: 152–153).

Toad magic and horse lore in East Anglia was associated with the Guild of Horsemen or the Society of the Horsemen's Word, whose members were known popularly as 'horse whisperers' and 'horse witches.' Membership of this rural, all-male secret society was supposed to give control over any untamed or aggressive horse by whispering the 'Word' in their ear. East Anglian folklorist George Ewart Evans said that in the Cambridgeshire fens this secret 'word of power' was *Siciubeo,* meaning 'I command' and it worked every time. While researching the horse whisperers working in the farming community of Suffolk, Evans became convinced that they could do what they claimed. He said they could stop a horse in its track and keep it there until they decided to release it. This was also a trick that witches could play. East Anglian folklorist C.F. Tebbutt writing in the 1940s implicitly linked the secret society with witches when he wrote; 'One form of witchcraft with no menace to others was the Horsemen's Guild. Members of this guild or cult had the power to control horses and claimed it came from the Devil. This power gave them a great advantage as farriers and horse breakers' (Tebbutt 1942).

After their initiation into the Horsemen's Word by a man dressed up in a horned mask and animal skins to represent the Devil the new member was given the 'Word' by his mentor or tutor in the society. He was told the esoteric aspect of the Horseman's Society was based on the symbolism of the biblical myth of Cain as the first horseman and ploughman. In East Anglia the training was divided into six grades after initiation. These were connected to the cycle of the agricultural calendar from ploughing and seeding in early spring to harvest time in the late summer, the making of bread and the corn spirit John Barleycorn, probably representing Cain. The grades and the times of the year were known as The Plough, The Seed, The Green Corn, The Yellow Corn, The Stones and The Resurrection.

As well as a toad or frog bone the horsemen would use what was called a 'milt' or 'melch.' This was a small oval shaped piece of fleshy material taken from a foal's mouth after birth. Usually the animal swallows it so the horseman has to be quick enough to take it before that happens. Once safely secured it was then wrapped in thin white paper and placed in a baking tin. This was put in an oven that was not too hot until it went hard. It was then powdered, mixed with virgin olive oil and baked again. The resulting material was placed in a muslin bag and held under the horsemen's arm to absorb his sweat. It could then be used as a magical charm to calm and control horses.

Along with this form of horse magic was the practical use of 'jading' or 'drawing' oils. The recipes for these oils were given to the new member of the Horseman's Word after their initiation. Those who were knew the secrets of the jading and drawing oils were called 'horse witches' as it was popularly regarded as a form of witchcraft. The 'magic' of these materials depended to a large extent on the sensitive sense of smell that horses have. The oils were split into those that smelt obnoxious or unpleasant and those which had a pleasant scent. Both worked equally well for controlling and calming wayward horses or taming wild ones.

George Ewart Evans said that the easiest way to stop a difficult horse bolting from a stable was to rub the doorpost with a dead mole. Cat's urine and pepper had the same effect. A horse could also be stopped from leaping over a stable's half-door by rubbing bay leaves and cuckoo-pint flowers on it. An effective jading oil with rather nasty ingredients was made from the dried and powdered livers of a stoat and a rabbit. These were added to the natural plant resin often used by witches with the evocative name of 'dragon's blood'. Another recipe was a mixture of dried rue, feverfew and hemlock powdered in a pestle and mortar and made into a paste. Crushed aniseed and fennel seeds were also used to attract and calm down horses. Other jading oils contained aromatic herbs such as rosemary, cinnamon and oregano. These were used in distilled form as essential oils and a few drops were applied directly to the horse's skin. They were also wafted under their nostrils using a cloth, handkerchief or cotton wool or baked into small oat cakes or gingerbread and fed to the animal. Some members of the Society of the Horsemen used a powerful combination of essential oils, the magical Word and the toad bone amulet.

Arthur Randall, who has a young man worked on a farm in Norfolk, recounted a meeting in 1911 with a member of the Horseman's Word who demonstrated his powers. The horseman asked Randall if he had ever seen the Devil and when he replied in the negative the man said he had many times. He then thrust a two-pronged pitchfork into a dung heap and harnessed a horse to it. The man commanded the animal to pull but however it strained it could not remove the fork. Then the horseman muttered something under his breath and 'released it' and the fork came out easily. The man warned Randall not to tell anyone what he had seen and swore him to secrecy (Randall 1966:109–110). It is possible that by asking Randall if he seen the Devil the horseman was testing the young man to see if he was a fellow member of the Word. If he was then he would have encountered a horseman dressed as Old Hornie at his initiation into the guild.

Another rural secret society that was sometimes connected to the Horseman's Word was the sinister Order of Bonesmen. Members carried the knucklebone from either a sheep or a human hand as a sign of their association with the group. Among their occult practices was the drinking of a potion made from cremated and powdered human bones mixed with wine or ale. The drinking of this was supposed to induce visions of the spirit world. This was because part of the dead person's spirit essence was still retained in their remains and connected them to the afterlife. The Bonesmen also practised another necromantic rite that involved playing a flute carved from a human bone to call up the shades of the dead. This may be connected to toad magic as the modern cunning man and Toadman Andrew D. Chumbley described carving a toad bone to make a flute for the magical purpose of necromancy (see his book on the toad bone rite called *One: The Grimoire of the Golden Toad*).

The members of the Horseman's Word could immobilize horses and some East Anglian female witches in East Anglia also had that power. In the late 19th century riders and drivers of horse-drawn vehicles used to avoid passing a cottage on the crossroads at Langstanton. It was inhabited by a witch called Bet Cross who would stop horses and they would only go when she decided to release them. When the drivers tried to make them move by using their whips Old Bet would cry out: 'Ain't no good beating them horses because they can't go till I let's them!'

At Histon (Cambridgeshire) in the early 1900s a woman in the village was waiting for the weekly grocer's cart to call so she could buy some flour. When he arrived she was surprised when he passed by her house without stopping as he usually did. She shouted after the driver and he said she would have to wait for two hours while he did other urgent deliveries.

When the grocer eventually arrived back at the woman's house she swore at him and shut the door in his face. When he got back on his cart the horse refused to go. Nothing he did would persuade it to move an inch. The witch, for that is what she was, opened the door and began laughing: 'You made me wait while my fire went out, so now you can just wait too.' The grocer was stuck outside the cottage until the middle of the afternoon. Finally the witch came out and whispered in the horse's ear; 'All right, you can go now'. Immediately the animal galloped off down the road (Porter 1969:58).

Horses also feature in popular folk magic and there are indications this dates back to pagan beliefs about equine worship. In East Anglia this was associated with the Iron Age horse goddess Epona and with the Germanic god Woden, leader of the Wild Hunt on his eight-legged steed. Horse skulls were buried in the ground as sacrificial offerings and examples have also been found in pre-Roman holy wells at Chelmsford and Wickford in Essex. In medieval times and up to the present day horse skulls have been buried in the foundations of new buildings, including, bizarrely, Christian chapels, or placed in the ground at the liminal barrier of the front door as a protective amulet or charm.

W. H. Barrett told a story of a farm worker he knew as a young man called Enoch Clingoe. The old man used to tell tales in the pub about two spectral white horses that haunted a nearby Army rifle range. They were supposed to have belonged to an Iron Age chieftain who had fought a battle on the site against the Roman legions when they invaded southern Britain. Clingoe used to visit the firing range secretly after dark with a wheelbarrow collecting spent bullets. He then sold them to a scrap metal dealer who paid him for their lead content. On one visit Clingoe was digging for bullets when he came across what he thought was an old lump of iron. When he got it home and cleaned the earth off the object he discovered it was a small statue of a man with a horse's head. After Clingoe died the image of this horse-god was sold at auction to a man from the horseracing town of Newmarket in Suffolk. The proceeds from the sale were used to pay for the old man's wake and funeral and he was seen off in great style (Barrett 1964:34–39).

In pagan Norse magic a horse skull was placed on a *nithstong* or pole and used as part of a deadly cursing ritual. The skull was pointed towards the intended victim's house or direction. It was then used as a medium or focus for the sorcerer to send them malefic thoughts and negative energy. As has been seen above, horse skulls were also used magically for protective reasons and as apotropaic charms for averting evil forces. They were placed on the gables and outside walls of houses and on fences and gateposts to protect against demons and the power of witchcraft. The Folk Museum in Cambridge has a collection of horse remains recovered from old buildings during renovation and demolition. They include a jawbone that was hidden in the wall cavity of a 17th century house. Similar exhibits are on display in the Museum of Witchcraft at Boscastle in Cornwall.

At Bungay (Suffolk) another house from the same period had no less then forty horse skulls ritually deposited under its floor. Obviously its occupants felt in need of a lot of magical protection. In the early 1980s a builder renovating a 17th century cottage in Manuden (Essex) came across an old bread oven set in a wall that had been sealed up and plastered over in either the 18th or 19th century. When he opened it there was a horse skull inside. He tried to preserve it by putting it in a cardboard box but it was very brittle. Unfortunately it broke into pieces and was thrown away. Another horse skull charm was found in an old cottage at South Ockendon. It had been secreted between a chimney flue and two adjoining walls.

At Market Hill in Huntingdon a horse skull was used in an annual folk ceremony of 'beating the bounds.' It was carried around the boundary of the land belonging to the Freemen of the town. At certain places a hole was dug in the ground and a boy was briefly placed head down in it. Freeman from the town of Godmanchester sometimes turned up and attempted to wrest the horse's skull away from their rivals. Nigel Pennick has suggested this folk tradition was a far memory of pagan horse and human sacrifices (1986:6).

Considering it was the survival of a pagan magical custom it is strange horse skulls have been found in the foundation of Christian religious buildings. In 1897 at Littleport in the Cambridgeshire fens when a new Methodist chapel was built a horse's head was buried in its foundations. The leader of the builders' gang sent his nephew to get the head from a local abattoir. A trench was dug and the center of it was marked with a wooden stake driven into the ground. The skull was then placed in the hole and the chief builder poured a libation of beer over it 'for luck and to drive the Devil away.' The ritual was justified by saying it was 'an old heathen custom' to get rid of evil spirits. Animal blood obtained from a butcher's shop was also mixed with mortar in new houses in East Anglia for the same reason and suggests another relic of former pagan sacrifices.

Horse magic also survived in the popular belief that horseshoes were protective amulets and talismans that attracted good fortune. To be effective they had to be placed in position with the 'horns' upwards. If reversed then it was believed their protective power was negated and the 'luck' they attracted would 'run out' into the ground. They were supposed to represent the crescent moon and as such were a symbol of the Roman lunar goddess of hunting and the woods, Diana. The horseshoe was supposed to protect the house and its inhabitants from the influence of evil spirits and the spells of black witches. At Staninfield in Suffolk a representation of a horseshoe was carved on a tile in the porch 'to keep the Devil out.'

In 1855 *Brad's Popular Antiquities* described how a carpenter in Ely suddenly became seriously ill. Suspicion fell on a woman he had evicted from a property he owned. His friends agreed that the only way he could be saved was to send for the local blacksmith. They asked him to make a three brand new horseshoes and these were fixed to the patient's front door. This was designed to keep the witch away and negate her power over the sick man. Despite these protective devices the witch managed to enter the house and the man's bedroom to torment him further. It was then found out to save money the smith had supplied three donkey shoes instead of making new horseshoes and they did not work (Porter 1962: 182).

In 1863 the Reverend Hugh Pigot met a woman from Hadleigh in Essex who like many of those in the village believed in witchcraft. She told the clergyman about a young woman who became sick and the doctor did not know what was wrong with her. Her parents believed an elderly woman who often visited the house was responsible for their daughter's condition. A new horseshoe was placed above the front door to prevent the witch or her fetch (spirit double) entering the house. Soon afterwards when the woman's visits had ceased because of the protective charm the patient recovered.

Another apotropaic device used by horsemen and farmers in East Anglia was a flint stone with a natural hole in it. This was known as a hag stone or witch stone and a piece of iron such as an old key was attached to it with a cord or string. It was then hung up in a stable as a charm to protect the horses from being 'hag ridden' or 'night ridden' by witches or faeries. The Good Folk were supposed to be frightened of iron. An 18th century source said that the ignorant believed that horses were ridden at night by sprites and hobgoblins because they find them sweating in the morning and their manes and tails tangled. George Ewart Evans told a story about a Suffolk about a man whose mare was getting disturbed and upset during the night. Friends recommended him to hang a round flint with a hole in it from a wire in the stable. Next morning when the owner went to check on his horse it was quiet and calm. The hag stone was also used in East Anglia as an amulet to ward off the Evil Eye and Evans compares it to the ancient symbol of the All-Seeing Eye painted on Sicilian boats for the same purpose (1974: 181–184). Modern traditional witches use hag stones to achieve visionary dreams during which they travel to the Otherworld and communicate with spirits.

In the 20th century there was a traditional coven operating in a Norfolk village that was led by a woman called Monica English. She was also briefly a member in the early 1960s of the Wiccan coven run by Gerald B. Gardner in Hertfordshire. English had allegedly joined it to find out what he was doing. This was because members of her coven believed that Gardner was bringing witchcraft into disrepute with his sensational publicity-seeking activities According to the writer Cottie Burland, who worked at the British Museum and knew Monica English, a former Magister or 'master' of this group was also a Roman Catholic. The coven was supposed to have venerated Epona, the Celtic horse goddess. Several of the coven members were associated with the local fox hunt and rode horses to their meeting place. According to one source they actually included the animals in some way in their rites and magical workings (pers.com Michael Clarke).

As in other parts of the British Isles, the hare was regarded in East Anglian folklore as a magical animal associated with witches. It was a form taken by their familiars and when they shapeshifted. The species *lepus* is at least three million years old and the Mountain Hare found in Britain can be traced back at least 100,000 years. It flourished in the interglacial period alongside the hippopotamus, woolly rhinoceros, cave bears, saber-toothed tigers, mammoths and early humans. The more common Brown Hare that lives in eastern England was introduced into Britain as late as the Bronze or Iron Age.

Although the hare is sometimes called the jackrabbit in the United States, it is very different from the common rabbit. It is bigger, has longer ears, an elongated body and powerful hind legs. Unlike rabbits, baby hares are born with fur and with their eyes open.

They are therefore able to fend for themselves much earlier then the offspring of rabbits. The hare's strong back legs mean they can run at speeds in excess of 45 miles per hour and leap eight feet forward or high. The unusual position of their eyes situated almost on the side of their head means they have a remarkable 380 degree vision.

In mythology and folklore all over the world the hare is a symbol of fertility and associated with the moon and springtime. The hare's significance as an emblem of fecundity is based on the scientific fact that they can conceive while still pregnant. Hares were once believed to lay eggs and hatch their young. For this reason they appear in the creation myths of several religions worldwide and are the bearer of the Cosmic Egg of creation. In Western folklore the hare became the Easter Bunny associated with the giving of chocolate eggs at the spring festival, possibly through the custom being imported by German emigrants to the United States.

The hare was an animal associated with several European pagan goddesses such as the Nordic Freya, the Celtic Ceridwen and Andrastre, the Roman Diana, the Greek Artemis and the Germanic Holda. Writing in the 8th century CE the clerical historian the Venerable Bede linked the name of a Saxon hare-headed goddess Eostre whom allegedly gave her name to the Christian festival of Easter. In turn her name is said to have derived from the goddess of the dawn Aurora. Her mother was the Germanic earth goddess Jord and in Germany stone altars, known later in Christian times as 'Easter stones,' were erected for her worship. Until the custom was banned in the 19th century, young people decorated these stones with wild flowers and danced around them at Easter time. This sounds suspiciously like a far memory of a pagan fertility ritual performed in the spring.

In the Iron Age the hare was regarded as a magical animal by the ancient Britons. It is recorded that Boudicca, the warrior queen of the Iceni tribe in what is now modern Norfolk, used a pet hare for divination during her revolt against the Roman occupation forces. She released the animal from under her cloak and sent it towards the ranks of Roman troops. Boudicca then observed whether the hare ran towards the assembled legions or away towards her army to divine if they would be victorious or defeated in the battle.

It was widely believed that witches could transform themselves into animals and their favorite form for shapeshifting was the hare. In the old days in Cambridgeshire country people would not eat hare-pie because they might be 'eating a witch.' There is recurring motif in folk tales from all over the British Isles of witch-hares being hunted down and shot. The hunter or hunters then follow the blood trail and find an injured woman who has an identical wound on her body or is dead. This belief that a witch can change shape into lupine form has an ancient history. The Irish legend of the hero Ossian or Oisin tells how the Celtic warrior was out hunting one day. His pack of hounds disturbed a larger-than-normal hare and chased it for miles across the countryside. Oisin knew there was something strange and unearthly about the animal as one side of it was colored gold and the other silver. Oisin managed to wound the animal in one of its back legs and the injured hare sought refuge in a large bunch of reeds.

When the warrior went to finish it off the creature had vanished. Instead he saw an oak door in the ground. He opened the door and went down a stone stairway into a large underground hall. At one end, sitting on a high-backed chair made of solid silver, was the most beautiful woman Oisin had ever seen. He realized she was the Queen of the Sidhe—the faery folk. However he was horrified to see blood pouring down her leg from a deep gash. It corresponded to the injury Oisin had inflicted on the hare and he begged her forgiveness for his mistake.

In Norfolk there is a story about a witch-hare and Queen Anne Boleyn, the mother of Queen Elizabeth I and one of his unfortunate wives beheaded on the orders of King Henry VIII. When he wanted to end his marriage with Boleyn, the king had her charged with adultery and witchcraft. The popular, if false, belief that she had been born with six fingers on one hand supported this allegation. This deformity was regarded as a clear sign she was a witch and was enough to condemn her to death. Because of her royal status Boleyn was executed with an axe rather than hanged with a rope.

Anne Boleyn's ancestral home was at Blickling in Norfolk and her ghost was supposed to haunt the nearby family church at Salle. After she was executed in 1536 Boleyn's body was buried in an old chest in unconsecrated ground at the Tower of London. A local legend in Blickling says that family retainers were sent London to secretly dig up the body and they took it back to Norfolk. It was then reburied at Salle church alongside Boleyn's other ancestors.

In 1924 the verger at Salle, James Clement, decided to challenge and disprove the story that the ghost of the dead queen haunted the church and churchyard. He went there after dark on a night of the full moon when she was supposed to appear. He sat in one of the pews opposite where the body of Anne Boleyn was reburied and waited. Nothing happened, but just as he was leaving the church he paused at the door. It was bright moonlight and almost as clear as day. Suddenly Clements saw a large hare loping up the path. It ran past him and through the open door into the church. The verger went back into the building and tried to chase the hare out. They circled the church twice and then as the animal went around the font for the second time Clements tripped and fell. As he was getting up the hare rushed past him and out of the half-open door. He immediately ran outside but there was no sign of the animal. When the verger was telling his story to George Ewart Evans he indicated that he thought the appearance of the hare was connected to Anne Boleyn. Clements also added that he had been born during the 'chiming hours' of the night and such people were supposed to have the psychic gift of the Second Sight (1972:167–168).

Although it was generally considered very unlucky to injure or kill a hare, probably in case it was a witch in disguise and she would curse or haunt the offender, its body parts were widely used in popular folk magic. For instance, if a person carried a hare's foot it was believed to prevent rheumatism, arthritis and cramp. If someone already had these health conditions the hare foot would help to alleviate the symptoms. Actors also carried them to improve their memory for remembering lines and enhance their acting skills.

If a pregnant woman carried a hare foot it would prevent a miscarriage. The baby would not be born with the facial disfigurement popularly called a harelip and the child would be strong and virile. However if the pregnant woman saw a large hare in the countryside and it crossed her path the baby could be born deformed. This was because the animal might be a witch in disguise. The brain of a hare, dried, mixed with wine and taken before bed, prevented oversleeping. Because of its fertile powers the genitals of a buck (male) hare were thought to be a powerful aphrodisiac and used by witches in love spells.

Hares were not the only creatures whose form witches used for shapeshifting. W. Barrett gave an account of Hallowe'en has it was celebrated and experienced by a young boy in the fens in the early 1800s. Osier twigs and black chicken feathers were placed at the doors and windows of farm buildings on that haunted night to ward off the local witches and evil spirits coming from the fens. A plate of thick slices of ham and a loaf of bread were also put outside the farmhouse door 'to feed the dead', who were said to roam abroad on this night that in country districts heralded the beginning of the winter.

There was also a custom for the oldest man and the youngest boy in the household to go around the house and the outbuildings before midnight with a lantern to check that all was well. The boy in Barrett's account accompanied his eldest uncle and they went to the orchard to check on the apple trees and the beehives. An owl flew low over the couple emitting a loud screech and the old man managed to hit it with his walking stick and it fell dead to the ground. He told the boy: 'That's one old witch that won't go home tonight.'

When the pair got back to the house the boy's aunt threw a handful of sulphur on the fire to stop the witches disguised as owls from coming down the chimney. His uncle added to this by tossing a bag of gunpowder used in his gun on the flames. There was a loud bang and everyone was covered in soot. When the smoke cleared a dead jackdaw that had been in the chimney was lying dead on the aunt's lap. It was agreed that another witch had come to a deadly end.

As the old grandfather clock chimed at the witching hour of midnight the boy and his uncle went out to do their final patrol around the farm. In the orchard they found a dead mouse, still warm, lying on top of one of the beehives. The uncle collected the bodies of the dead owl and the mouse. When they got back to the house he threw them and the jackdaw on the fire. He commented to his nephew: 'Three witches on one Hallowe'en isn't a bad bag' (Barrett 1964:133–136).

A witch was often seen wandering the fens at night when decent God-fearing folk were safely tucked up in bed. After her wanderings farmers reported that when they went to collect their cows in the morning they had been milked overnight. Four young farmers who had been drinking at a wedding party and were full of bravado decided to prove that the witch was responsible for the nocturnal milking. They went to her cottage and looking through the grimy window saw the old woman surrounded by cats. She then began to play on a whistle and two snakes, each at least four feet long, slid into the room.

They reared up on their tails and swayed in time to the music. As the young men watched fascinated the witch wrapped herself in a long black cloak and left the house, followed behind closely by the cats and the two snakes. The men tracked her across the fields at a distance to a neighboring farm owned by the father of one of the young farmers. They watched as the witch entered a field and approached the cows in it. The owner of the farm was alerted and let loose his prize bull into the field. The witch fled with the cats and snakes fast behind her. The cows were never milked again at night. However, the next year when the farmer cut the field for hay he found and killed two of the biggest snakes he had ever seen.

7

Charms and Spells

THE USE BY witches and sorcerers of charms for healing and for cursing goes back to prehistory. In eastern England so-called 'elf bags' have been found by archaeologists in graves dating from the Anglo-Saxon period. These charm bags contained dried herb, copper and silver coins, sometimes engraved with 'pagan' equal-armed crosses, small pieces of black and white flint and prehistoric arrowheads, popularly known as 'elf bolts' or 'elf shot' and used by witches to 'blast' their enemies. Similar magical pouches date back to the Iron and Bronze Ages.

In the historical and early modern period in East Anglia, as elsewhere, many of the spoken and written charms were based on Christian, usually pre-Reformation, forms. The Essex witch Elizabeth Lowys was said in 1564 to have issued curses by calling on Jesus and threatening him: 'Christ, my Christ, if thou be my Saviour come down and avenge me of my enemies or thou shalt not be my Saviour.' In 1613 one non-conformist preacher in Essex noted rather ironically that the standard of Christian worship among local people was so poor that 'only witches and sorcerers use the Lord's Prayer.'

The Essex preacher George Gifford told of knowing a woman who was scared of faeries. She wore a charm bag tied around her neck containing a piece of parchment with a verse from the Gospel of St John written on it. Other popular witchcraft and anti-witchcraft charms were also of a Christian origin and they were usually based on Roman Catholicism. They included salt that had been blessed and consecrated by a priest, bottles filled with holy water and beeswax candles stolen from a church, the sacramental host and the sign of the cross. Such items were used by both witches and people seeking to combat their alleged malefic powers. Because of the fear of witchcraft the lids to baptismal fonts were locked in country churches and communion wafers were placed in a sealed metal box.

Dr William Bullen was the Anglican rector of Blaxhall in Suffolk before moving to London where he changed career and became a surgeon. In his book *Defence Againste Sicknesse, Sorres and Woundes* (1562) he wrote about a 'false witche' he had known called Mother Line. She was consulted by mothers when their children were sick and cured them using a 'string of ebony beads' (i.e., a Catholic rosary) from the Holy Land and 'certain words.' People also went to the witch to have 'the Faerie charmed and sprytes conjured away.' Dr Bullen intervened in these activities and confiscated the rosary. He said that all those who used such witchcraft charms should be burnt at the stake because they were enemies of God (Wright 2004:8–9).

Another witch the doctor knew was Mother Didge of Kershall. She also used a Catholic rosary and a wax candle to cure burns and a complaint known as St Anthony's Fire, possibly a burning skin rash. In her healing the witch would recite the following well-known charm:

There came three angels
out of the north-east,
One brought fire,
The other frost,
Out fire,
In frost,
In the Name of the Father,
Son and Holy Ghost.

Another popular charm was used to heal burns and also stop bleeding was:

Stand fast, ire as Christ did,
When he was crucified on the cross,
Blood remains in the veins,
As Christ did in all his pains.

A charm to remove a thorn and prevent it from infecting the patient was as follows:

Jesus of a maid was born,
He was pricked with thorn,
No more shall this by Christ, Our Lord,
Lord bless what I have said,
 So be it unto thee as I have said,
Amen, Amen, Amen

W. H. Barrett told a story about a gypsy woman who sold charms to the women in the fens. She visited the homes of clergymen and begged them to give her old prayer books and Bibles they longer wanted. If they complied with her request she then tore out the pages and made small bags out of them. These were packed with sand and earth and tied with red wool. The gypsy woman sold these charms to the fen women to protect them from the evil power of witchcraft (1964:51).

Keith Thomas has said that while there were no specific charms for such daily tasks as reaping corn or milking cows, except for anti-witchcraft counter-charms, when farmers were dependent on factors or circumstances outside of or beyond their control they would employ magical precautions. He cites as examples traditional fertility customs that had a Christian veneer but were evidently pagan in origin, e.g., burying a piece of cake in the first furrow that is ploughed as an offering to 'Mother Earth', or rural seasonal customs such as wassailing the apple orchards on Twelfth Night, blessing the plough before spring sowing, midsummer bonfires and the making of corn dollies at harvest time. Thomas cites the wife of a smith at Colchester who practised a magical ritual that made people think they had a lucky plough. There were also charms to get rid of weeds in cornfields, magical formulae to keep insect pests and vermin like rats and mice away from crops stored in barns and to bring fertility to the land (Thomas 1991:775–776).

Quite a lot of the witch's work concerned love affairs and marital matters. In 1617 when the wife of John Redman of Sutton in Cambridgeshire left him for another man he traveled all over the county visiting wizards in an attempt to get her back (ibid:278). In 1818 a ritual to make a woman fall in love with a man was recommended by a witch in Newmarket: 'Take some new wax and some powdered bone from a male skeleton. Use it to make an image of the desired man during 'the hour of Mars and in the new moon. Then carve the image with the sigil of the Martian planetary spirit and if evoked it will bring about the result. For a man to love a woman use powdered bone from a female skeleton and evoke the Venusian spirit with its sigil at the hour of Venus.'

Despite having only one eye and ugly features, a witch from Burnt Fen, who was mentioned before for milk-stealing, was married five times. People suspected she used the magical art of fascination to attract her many husbands and witchcraft was involved as all died sudden or violent deaths. Then she met a sixth man who also wanted to marry her and his workmates teased him that he should not forget to make a will before the wedding. On the evening before his marriage to the witch the husband-to-be was seen drinking heavily in a local inn. He was turned out at closing time and was so drunk that, instead of walking down the track to his home, he fell into a water-field ditch and drowned. His body was found next morning by a worker at a steam-driven pump engine near the ditch used for draining the fens (Barrett 1964:112–114).

Some witch charms were concerned with fertility in more general terms. One classic example was the so-called Fitchingfield Sticks. In the 1940s a man called Dan Pedder inherited a 17th century cottage in the Essex village of Fitchingfield where he knew his relatives had once lived. While doing renovations before moving in to the old cottage he was surprised to discover a strange-looking wooden stick hidden in a wall cavity that had been plastered over. The stick had two coiled snakes carved around it going in different directions.

When Pedder made some enquiries he discovered one of his ancestors, Goofy Mumford, had lived in the cottage in the 1780s. She was the village schoolmistress and many people believed she was a witch. When it was discovered she was teaching the girls about witchcraft after school she was beaten and stoned by an angry mob. As a result of the attack she subsequently died of her injuries. Pedder then found another stick hidden under the cottage thatch. It had images of birds, bees, rabbits, butterflies, wild flowers, a bull and three cows burnt into its surface. It was suggested by folklore experts that the first stick was used by the witch for healing and the second for increasing fertility (Young, 1993).

Although due to human nature it got less publicity then cursing, many witches specialized in healing. In Anglo-Saxon England so-called 'healer's knives' have been found among grave goods. These had handles made of ox horn with three brass nails hammered into them. They were also decorated on the handle and the blades with letters from the magical runic alphabet of Germanic origin. It is not known exactly what these knives were used for although archeologists have speculated it was for blood-letting or perhaps cutting healing herbs for simples or medical remedies. They could have also been used for sacrifices. Whatever their end these weapons definitely had a magical significance.

One healing ritual recommended by East Anglian cunning folk to cure a fever was, according to John Glyde, a survival 'of the sacrificial rites offered to the powers of darkness [sic] by the pagan Saxons and Danes' (1872:33). The patient was told to place their nail and toe parings and a lock of hair with a piece of raw beef in an earthenware pot. A black silk cloth was then tied over the mouth of the vessel. This was then buried in the center of a remote wood. As the meat slowly rotted so it was believed the fever would break and the sick person would be cured.

Joan Warden of Stapleford, Cambridgeshire was accused in 1582 of being a cunning woman. She vehemently denied the charge and said that she did not use any charms 'like a cunning person'. However she did admit to making up and prescribing ointments and potions made from 'healing herbes' to cure many diseases. If charged with practicing witchcraft people often tried to escape prosecution by saying they did not use written or spoken charms as that was illegal.

One method of healing used by witches and cunning folk in England and Wales was 'taking the measure.' A cunning woman called Elizabeth Mentlock from Cambridge, confessed in 1566 to diagnosing illness by measuring a band or girdle worn by her patient. She also used the method for people who came to her claiming they were haunted by a ghost or faery. Mentlock measured the piece of clothing from her elbow to her thumb (a biblical measurement known as a cubit) and if 'the band will be shorter and her cubit will reach further then it normally do' then the illness was definitely caused by a supernatural agency. When 'taking the measure' the wise woman always prayed to God and to St Charity. She also repeated the Lord's Prayer five times for the five wounds of Christ on the cross, five Ave Marias for Our Lady, and the Creed for the Father, Son and Holy Ghost and the Twelve Apostles. In 1592 Matilda Allin of Dullingham in Cambridgeshire was prosecuted for carrying handkerchiefs and girdles she had been given by sick people and 'measuring' pigs that were suffering from swine fever.

Some learned East Anglian cunning folk like James Murrell used astrology for healing purposes, especially diagnosis. This usually involved drawing up the patient's birth chart but also an image called the Zodiac Man. This figure was usually cut out from the cheap astrological almanacs sold in the 18th and 19th century. It was the classical depiction of a naked man standing with his legs apart and his arms upraised to form the magical symbol of a pentagram or five-pointed star. The figure was surrounded by a circle with the zodiac signs around its edge. Arrows or lines came from the signs and indicated the areas on the human body that they ruled. This diagram was widely used by witches and cunning folk to diagnose illness and diseases and find suitable herbal medicines to cure them (Davies 1999:154).

At his trial for fraud a Norfolk cunning man, James Stagg, whose day job was as a stonemason, openly boasted about his healing powers. He told the magistrates he had successfully treated people who had been told by doctors they were incurable (*The Times*, January 13th 1877). In the 1890s at Clapton, Suffolk a charmer called Mrs Bunn was renowned for healing burns. She told people she had inherited the skill from her mother and the procedure was to bless the burn and moisten it with her saliva. Since Anglo-Saxon times human saliva has been regarded as an antiseptic healing agent. Mrs Bunn also recited 'certain unknown words' (an oral charm) under her breath when she was doing this. Even the local minister went to the charmer when he burnt his hand badly (Gurdon 1833).

Talking about the essential role of the village nurse, midwife and layer-out of the dead in East Anglia, folklorist Enid Porter said that before the establishment of the National Health Service in 1948 they were often the only medical help in fenland villages. Porter claimed that as well as orthodox medicine these practitioners also used herbal remedies and semi-magical cures. Some however were feared by local people because they also believed to practice 'the blacker arts of witchcraft' (Porter in Barrett 1964:5).

As well as healing East Anglian witches and cunning folk offered divinatory services. One popular form of divination was the 'Bible and the key.' It was widely used to divine the identity of thieves and the name of a future lover or partner. A large key was inserted in the Bible at the Book of Ruth or between the six and seventh verses of the last chapter of the *Song of Solomon*. The Bible was tied together with a ribbon worn in their hair or one of the enquirer's garter. The point being that it had to be an intimate object in daily contact with the querant's body. She and another woman suspended the Bible from the end of the garter or ribbon using the bow of the key. Each letter of the alphabet was then repeated until the initial of the future lover was reached. Then the Bible would spin around of its own accord. If this did not happen when the entire alphabet had been recited then the enquirer was doomed not to marry and would die a spinster. Another method of biblical divination practised by witches was to close their eyes and open the book at random. With their eyes still closed they pointed at a verse and then interpreted it to provide answers to their clients questions or offer advice to guide them through the day.

Witches have always been held responsible for bad or unusual storms by using magical rituals to create them. An entry in the parish records of Wells-next-the-Sea on the Norfolk coast in 1583, five years before the Spanish Armada, reported the drowning of thirteen sailors during a fierce storm at sea. The report claimed that the deaths of the men had been caused by the 'detestable working of an execrable witche of Kings Lynn.' She was named as Old Mother Gabley and had allegedly raised the storm by simply boiling thirteen eggs, one for each dead sailor, in a pail of water (*Norfolk Archaeology* V, 1859).

In the 1850s a woman called Old Mother Moore used to 'sell the wind' to sailors and fishermen on the quay at Leigh-on-Sea in Essex. She was described in unflattering terms as 'dirty, gaunt and ugly, with claw-like hands.' The witch accosted seamen preparing to set off from the harbor begging: 'Buy a fair wind, buy a fair wind.' Most of the men humored the old woman or from a superstitious belief in her powers gave her a few coins for insurance. Their attitude was it did not harm and it was better to be safe than be sorry. A similar custom was carried out by witches in the fishing port of Boscastle in north Cornwall that is today the site of a witchcraft museum.

One day a foreign captain who did not know about the custom refused to give Mother Moore any money and laughed in her face. He dismissed her claim to be able to control the wind as 'superstitious nonsense' and told his men to cast off the boat. As it left the harbor the strong wind that had been blowing suddenly stopped and the boat's sails fell limp. Dark clouds swept across the blue summer sky and it seemed as if night had fallen prematurely. Thunder and lightning was followed by heavy rain that flooded the deck of the boat. The terrified crew cried out in panic that it was 'the witch's work' and they were all going to be drowned.

Despite his initial skepticism about her powers, the captain picked up an axe and told his men: 'Fear not, I will kill the old witch!' He went to the front of the boat and struck the prow with several heavy blows with the axe. Almost immediately the storm abated, the clouds cleared, the sun came out and a strong wind carried the boat out of the harbor. Shortly afterwards it is alleged that Old Mother Moore was found dead. On her forehead were several deep gashes as if made with a heavy sharp instrument (Morgan 1973:46–47).

It was a common belief that some people possessed the power of the 'Evil Eye' and could curse by just looking at someone intensely. It was even said a sideways glance could 'blast' (injure or kill) humans and animals. This witch power was known as 'owl blinking' or 'owl blasting', presumably because unlike others the bird has large prominent eyes that face forward. In 2008 a psychiatrist, Dr Colin Ross, published a scientific paper called 'The Electro-physical Basis of Evil Eye Belief' in the *Journal of the American Anthropological Association*. Dr Ross said he had modified ECG neurofeedback equipment and claimed to have detected 'human ocular extramissions' or beams of energy emitted by the eye. He said that further experiments and research would be needed to see if this ocular energy could be harnessed through focused attention.

An old man who lived at North Walsham in Norfolk in the 1870s was said to possess the Evil Eye. One day a careless farm worker nearly knocked him down with a team of horses he was driving down the road. The old man stood one leg, closed one eye and glared hard at him with the other and then walked on. The next day the farm worker was in the fields and had an urge to look at his pocket watch. It was 11 am, the same time as he had encountered the old man in the lane. He immediately felt ill and nearly blacked out. This happened several days running and the man went to his doctor to find out what was wrong. The doctor prescribed some medicine and told him to take it five minutes before 11 o'clock and cross himself. The farm worker did this and the fainting fits stopped.

It was believed witches could curse people by sending a familiar spirit to injure or kill them, by obtaining the victim's nail parings, hair, blood or other bodily fluids, some material object belonging to them like a handkerchief or piece of jewellery, the use of poppet, a doll or image made of wax, wool or rags, or just by physical contact. At the trial of Elizabeth Bennett, one of the St Osyth witches, in 1582 a witness, William Bonner, claimed his wife and the defendant were 'familiar friends' and used to accompany each other everywhere. Bonner said that the witch visited her friend and enquired tenderly after her health. She then hugged his wife and kissed her full on the lips. Immediately the woman's lips swelled up and her eyes sank into her head (Rosen 1991:120–121).

In 1602 a Norfolk woman, Mary Woods, was asked by one of her clients, the wife of a doctor, to predict the date her husband would die. She also offered Woods 'a large reward' if she would use her herbal knowledge to poison him. The wise woman refused to have anything to do with the woman's plot to get rid of her unwanted spouse. In fact Woods seems to have concealed her magical activities from the authorities for many years by threatening to expose to the authorities many of her clients who wanted to have their husband murdered (Thomas 1991:287).

Susan Barker was arraigned at Chelmsford assizes in 1616 on the comparatively rare charge of practicing necromancy or the summoning up the spirits of the dead. She was described as a 'common witch seduced by the Devil.' It was said she had gone to the churchyard of the parish church at Upminster, dug up a grave and stolen a human skull. Barker had then used this grisly object in 'certain evil and devilish acts, charmes and sorceries' and in a spell to bewitch a woman she knew called Mary Stevens (Haining 1974:19–20). Human and animal skulls were often items used for magical purposes by witches and cunning people and displayed in their cottages.

At Kings Lynn in 1626 the Reverend Alexander Roberts described the activities of Mary Smith in his *A Treatise on Witchcraft*. Smith was known as 'a troublesome woman' because she had frequent arguments and disputes with her neighbors. They in turn accused her of bewitching them. When a sailor, John Orkton, hit Smith's son after the boy had annoyed him the alleged witch expressed the hope all his fingers would drop off. Orkton began complaining of sharp pains in his hands and feet. He contracted gangrene, lost his extremities and had to give up going to sea.

Mary Smith accused her neighbor Mrs Hancocke of stealing one of her hens. She said she hoped its bones would stick in her throat. The woman fell ill with fits and was cursed a second time after standing at Smith's door. Hancocke went to a local wizard and he sold her a charm and some 'magic powder.' This had to be baked into a cake with a few drops of her urine and carried on her person. Within a few days she recovered completely and Smith had no more power over her.

The witch then cursed a rather overweight servant girl employed by another neighbor. Smith rather unkindly called her a 'fat-tailed sow' and predicted she would not be overweight for long. The girl began to rapidly lose weight, became malnourished and was virtually wasting away. She was only saved from a painful and lingering death because she moved away to a place where apparently Smith's powers could not reach her. Another neighbor found a large toad and several crabs in his house. He was convinced that Mary Smith had sent them to attack and torment him. This was confirmed in his mind when he threw the toad on the fire. Witnesses said that at exactly that moment Mary Smith screamed out in pain. This did not solve the problem as the man began to suffer from loss of memory and had to give up his job.

In September 1660 crowds gathered in the streets of Bury St Edmunds after a plague of large spiders invaded the town. They watched spellbound as the creatures moved in a large mass towards the house of a former Member of Parliament called Duncombe. When the spiders arrived at his house they swarmed up the doorposts and spun a web from one side of the front door to the other. One of Duncombe's servants placed a bundle of dry straw under the spiders and lit it to destroy the creatures. His master believed witchcraft was behind the plague and a local coven of witches had sent them to his house because he had spoken out against them and their activities.

A thirteen-year-old boy, John Stockings, from Heaverland in Norfolk became ill and took to his bed. A physician was called to examine him and declared he could find nothing physically wrong with the boy. Shortly after the doctor's visit Mary Banister, a friend of the family, called at the house. She took the patient's hand and asked how he was feeling. After she had left Stockings told his parents: 'If I dies burn Goody Banister for she hath bewitched me bad.' She was brought to trial, but the magistrate refused to accept the evidence against her and acquitted Banister of any involvement in the boy's illness.

In Victorian times a cunning woman called Mother Hunsley lived at Burnt Fen and terrorized and extorted money from gullible people. She placed small mounds of earth from freshly dug graves on their doorsteps during the night. The next morning when the occupants of the house had discovered the deposits the cunning woman would call on them offering her help. She told them the Devil had put the earth on their doorstep and they were cursed. However if they paid her she would cast a spell to avert the evil influence. Many superstitious people were quite happy to hand over half a crown so the Old One would leave them alone (Porter 1969:166).

Mark Taylor passed on several stories about bewitching and cursing told to him by a Norfolk doctor in the 1920s. In one case a woman came to the surgery and asked the doctor if he could cure her of an unsightly lump on the back of her head. She explained that some years earlier her children quarreled with the children of a supposed witch. The woman came out of her house and hit her over the head with a hazel stick (wand?). From then on every spring the lump developed on her head and only went down with the sap in the autumn.

Another woman in the doctor's village believed she had been 'over-looked' by a local farmer who had the Evil Eye. When she placed milk in a bowl it always broke and if she put meat in the oven it always came out half-raw. She told the doctor she had counteracted the bewitchment by writing the Lord's Prayer on a piece of paper, soaking it until the ink ran and then drinking the water. Sadly she committed suicide six months later and left a letter blaming the farmer's magical persecution.

Taylor also came across a woman who was becoming mentally un-balanced and claimed she was bewitched. After her doctor visited her she found a brown paper parcel containing stones. She believed the doctor was putting a spell on her, although it was Taylor's opinion it was one of her neighbors, who was widely suspected locally of practicing witchcraft. He was consulted by a man who claimed his wife had put a curse on him. She had run off with her lover and before leaving had put a spell on her husband. The man claimed he was now impotent and unable to have sexual relations with any other woman. Taylor suggested that a priest should be called in to take the spell off using bell, book and candle (the traditional Rite of Exorcism). He had discovered this form of bewitchment was very common in medieval times when it was known in Latin as *vinculum* or 'restraint' (Taylor 1929:126–127).

Enid Porter described how in 1932 a Norfolk woman consulted a cunning woman who was known to tell fortunes and cast spells. She did this because she believed her husband was having a secret affair with an unknown younger woman. The wife paid the witch to put a curse on her husband's lover. This was to give her sores on her face so the man no longer found her attractive and also to identify herself. Two days later a young local woman came to her door. She had heard the wife had been to a witch and begged her to have the disfiguring rash on her face removed. If she did then she promised to have nothing more to do with her husband (1964:xv and 1974:157–158).

The use of the poppet, usually a wax image but sometimes a rag doll, has an ancient origin and was widespread in the practice of historical witchcraft. In 1981 a sensational newspaper headline claimed that 'devil dolls' had been discovered at an Essex hospital. It said horrified workmen had found a 'black magic shrine' with 'voodoo-like dolls' and a box of pins. There were two human effigies about four inches long made from rags, a piece of coal and some bits of animal bone. From their position the objects probably dated back to the 1850s when the hospital was a workhouse for the local poor (*The Southend Evening Echo*, 18th December 1981).

A classic case of the modern use of witch poppets occurred in the early 1960s in the historical Norfolk village of Castle Rising and its surrounding area. Once far closer to the sea then it is now, in 1138 William d'Albini built a castle on a prominent mound (possibly a former pagan site) and the medieval village developed around it. In 1330 Queen Isabella, known as the 'she-wolf' and the French wife of King Edward II, was imprisoned in the castle accused of his horrible murder with a red-hot poker. Her ghost is still supposed to haunt its ruins. From 1544 it was owned by the Howard family, the Dukes of Norfolk, who used it as a rather grand hunting lodge.

In September 1963 a bricklayer doing restoration on the castle made a sinister discovery when he arrived for work. Nailed to the ancient oak door of the castle were two seven-inch figures of a man and a woman made from pink modeling clay. The female one was pierced through the heart with a large hawthorn. Also nailed to the door next to the images was a sheep's heart with thirteen hawthorn twigs in it. On the ground below these objects was a circle of black soot containing small fragments of animal bones and nearby were a second circle and a cross. Nobody in the village claimed to know who was responsible and the police were baffled.

Four months later in January 1964 two teenage boys out for bicycle ride visited the remote Norman church of St James at Bawsey. They went inside the roofless ruin and were astonished to see a sheep's heart pierced with eleven hawthorn twigs nailed to the wall of the bell tower. Below it on the ground was a circle made from soot about eighteen inches in diameter. Inside it was a partly burnt down black candle that appeared to have been an ordinary household white one to which dye had been added. It presence led the police to jump to the conclusion that a Black Mass had been celebrated in the ruined church by 'devil-worshippers.'

The third in what was becoming a series of rituals took place in February 1964. This received national publicity because it took place on the royal estate at Sandringham owned by the Queen. It was at the ivy covered ruined church of St Felix on marshy ground next to the River Babblingley. It is the site of the first Christian church built in East Anglia and again was probably built at a place of former pagan worship. A teenage boy fishing on the river went into the church out of curiosity. He found another image of a woman made from pink modeling clay with her breast pierced with a hawthorn. Next to it was a sheep's heart with five hawthorn twigs in it. On the window ledge above it was the stub of a partly burnt black candle and on the ground below was the usual circle traced in soot.

The boy went back home and reported what he had found to his father. He drove back to look at the remains and then informed the police. The father was adversely affected by the find. He is supposed to have sat paralyzed at the wheel of his car before being able to drive to the police station. When he arrived he was in a state of collapse. It took him a full two days to recover from his experience at the church.

The final ritual was performed at Caister Castle in April 1964 and those responsible were nearly caught in the act. On the night of the full moon the custodian of the castle and his wife heard 'mysterious noises' at midnight when they were in bed, but they did not bother to get up and investigate. The next morning a family visiting the castle found an image made of pink modeling clay with a steel pin in its chest (gender unknown but it only had one leg), a sheep's heart and the usual circle of soot (*Gorleston Herald and East Norfolk Advertiser*, April 3rd 1964).

Although the local police investigated all three incidents as evidence of 'black magic rites' the person or persons responsible were never found. Rumors and gossip circulating in Castle Rising however suggested that local people knew who it was. The police consulted a local man called Frank Buckley, who the newspapers described as an expert on local folklore and witchcraft, about the first three rituals. After examining the objects found at Castle Rising he said his informed opinion was as the moon was waning at the time it was evidence of a 'death-ritual.' It had been performed by a young woman who had been crossed in love. He believed it was possible she had been taught the art of witchcraft by an older woman as part of an oral tradition in the area dating back centuries. According to Buckley, the sheep's heart represented the heart of the girl's lover who had left her for another woman. The male and female images were the two lovers and they had been pierced with the thorns so they would die. He regarded the circle of black soot as symbolic of the young woman's womb. Animal bones found in the circle represented the fact she was now sexless and barren since her lover had left her.

At Bawsey the ritual had been performed again while the moon was waning. Frank Buckley said that while the previous ritual had been designed to break up a relationship the latest was a love spell. Presumably the death-ritual had not worked and now the girl was invoking occult forces, melodramatically described by Buckley as the 'powers of darkness', to help get her boyfriend back. He interpreted the black candle as a phallic symbol placed in the circle to represent fertility. Buckley pointed out that the previous night had been St Agnes Eve when women traditionally performed divination rites so they could dream of their future lovers or life partners. He also suggested to the police that the person performing the rites might be mentally ill and in need of psychiatric help.

The final ritual that the police consulted the folklorist about was one on the Sandringham royal estate. Buckley said it looked from the exalted position of the black candle placed on the window ledge of the ruined church that the young woman had now succeeded in getting her lover back. The female image with the one leg indicated that she had overcome her rival and had triumphed. In fact the empty circle indicated she was now at peace with herself and content.

Although the police believed that the rituals had been carried out by only one person, and Frank Buckley had spoken at first of a young woman taught and guided by an older witch, the expert also hinted that others were involved in the background. In an interview with a local newspaper Buckley suggested the black candle used in the rituals may have also symbolized an absent warlock or witch-master, the 'man in black', of a coven. He said that Bawsey had a previous connection with witchcraft and that the police were also investigating a report of an old-style witch coven meeting near Norwich (Jones, April 1965).

Poppets were not only used for projecting negative energy at ex-lovers. Enid Porter mentioned the use of a wax image in the Cambridgeshire fens in the early 1900s. She said an old woman made an effigy of the South African politician Paul Kruger and stuck pins in it. This ritualistic act was to ensure the safe return of her sons and nephews who were fighting with the British army in the Boer War against the Afrikaner Dutch settlers (1964:xv).

In 1940 the staff from a medical research laboratory in London were evacuated to Cambridge to escape the German bombing in the Blitz. They were given temporary quarters in a building occupied by the University School of Anatomy. One day a student was fixing a broken light shield over an electric stove in the laboratory. He put his hand on top of one of the roof beams and found an object lying on it. It was a small image of a man made from clay or putty. When he reported the find he found out that the senior staff knew all about the image. They had left it in place 'for luck', especially in the prevailing wartime conditions (Porter 1969:397).

Various counter-charms were used to break spells, lift curses and nullify the power of witches and wizards. Some of these were quite dramatic in nature and are suggestive of former pagan sacrifices. In the 1660s an Essex farmer called Harcourt claimed his plough-horses and thirty of his cows had been bewitched. He was advised by a cunning man to burn one of the sick horses alive to break the curse and it worked. Writing eight years later an Essex vicar said it was commonplace in his parish for farmers to burn a pig or a chicken alive to counter-act bewitchment and 'drive the devils away.'

A cunning man in the early 1700s in Kings Lynn told the father of a girl who had been 'witched' to make a special cake to cure her. It was made from flour mixed with some of the victim's urine. The cunning man also gave the man an ointment 'like treacle' and a powder to put on the cake. There was also a piece of paper with 'certain words' written on it that had to be repeated during the baking. Once the cake was baked it was cut in half. One portion was to be placed on the front of the girl's body above her heart. The other was placed on her back directly opposite her heart (Davies 2003:110).

One traditional and popular method of breaking a witch's power over a bewitched person was known as 'scoring above the breath' i.e., making a small cut on the witch's face above her mouth, usually the nose or forehead, or sometimes on other parts of her body such as hands, arms and legs to draw blood. In 1769 Cambridge magistrates ordered William Adams of Grantchester to pay five guineas in compensation to Phoebe Haly of Caldicot. He had attacked and assaulted her in the belief she had bewitched him. Adams was also fined thirteen shillings by the court for his physical assault on the woman (*The Gentleman's Magazine*, 39, 1769).

In May 1808 Ann Izzard of Great Paxton in Cambridgeshire was attacked by her irate neighbors and badly injured. Several local women claimed she had bewitched them and as a result they had suffered fits. A mob broke into Izzard's cottage when her husband was absent and dragged her half-naked from her bed. Her arms were scratched with pins to draw blood and then she was beaten about the head and body with a piece of wood. When the mob left the cut and bruised woman managed to stagger to the new parish constable's house. The police officer refused to help her claiming he had not properly been sworn in.

In desperation Ann Izzard went to her widowed neighbor Alice Russell for help and she treated her wounds and put her to bed. Word reached the other villagers and they accused Russell of harboring and protecting witches. She was also attacked and beaten up and died later from shock and her injuries. The next day when the mob decided they would 'swim' Ann Izzard she fled to for her life to the next village. Subsequently nine of the villagers involved in the assaults on both women were sentenced to four weeks in prison (Davies 1999:111–12). In 1879 a man from Ething Green in Norfolk was arrested by the police for an assault on a sixteen-year-old girl. In his defense he said she was the daughter of a well-known 'bad old witch.' He claimed he had attacked the girl because she just as bad and had encouraged her mother in the practice of witchcraft (*Folklore Record* 2, 1879).

A witch called Miss Didsbury lived at Whitingham in the 1890s and was believed to have had the power over horses and other animals. One day two villagers were driving a herd of cows past her house when they suddenly stopped and would go no further. One of the herdsmen believed Miss Didsbury was responsible and she had cast a spell on the animals. He knocked at her front door and asked if he could have a match to light his clay pipe. When the old lady brought a box of matches to the door the man took out his penknife. Before she could get out of the way he lunged and nicked her on the forearm drawing a small amount of blood. This act of 'scoring' worked as immediately the cows awoke from their trance and carried on up the lane.

The Egyptologist and anthropologist Dr Margaret Alice Murray, who wrote two books on historical witchcraft that influenced the rise of modern Wicca, told of a case she had heard of 'scoring above the breath' in modern times. A Norfolk farmer had walked up to woman in the street and slashed her forehead with a knife. When brought before the magistrates' court on an assault charge the man said the victim was a witch. She had been to his farm begging and when he turned her away she threatened that he would have no butter in his churns to sell. This happened and when the farmer related the story to a friend he was advised to 'score the witch above the breath.' (quoted in Deacon 1976:51)

In the 1930s a Wisbech woman recounted how when her mother was a child she had ran up to a suspected witch and pricked her with a pin saying: 'I'm not scared of you!' The woman's husband also remembered an incident in the 1890s involving a man he knew who believed his prize sow had been bewitched. He asked the wife of a local horse-whisperer for advice and she identified the person responsible. She told him to cut the alleged witch's nose, wipe some of the resulting blood on a piece of paper and then burn it. He carried out her instructions and the sow not only recovered but it also gave birth to three healthy piglets (Porter 1874:160).

A suspected witch in the 1900s visited a farmer's wife on Christmas Eve while she was hanging up the seasonal evergreens. The woman forced herself into the kitchen demanding food and threatening to curse the household if she was not fed well. Unfortunately the witch sat down on a chair where the farmer's wife had left a large sprig of holly for the Yuletide decorations. She leapt into the air with a howl of pain clutching her bleeding buttocks and fled from the house. When the farmer's wife told her husband what had happened he laughed and said if a knife was not available then a sprig of holly served just as well 'to draw the blood of a witch' (Porter 1969:178). In fact holly was regarded in country folklore as a magical plant with protective powers. People planted it outside their front doors to prevent lightning strikes on the house—and keep out witches.

In the old days in Cambridgeshire farming people believe that if you drew blood from a bewitched animal it would be released from the power of the witch. One day a woman who lived in Horseheath was feeding her two hogs when a known witch passed by. She patted one of the animals on the head and casually remarked how good it looked. When she had gone on her way the pig stopped feeding and as a result dramatically lost weight. Its owner cut a small piece of flesh from its ear and tail in an attempt to make it well. Unfortunately it did not work because the woman did not burn them as she should have done and the pig died (Porter 1974:159).

Various types of charms were known in East Anglia to ward off witches and avert evil influences. A popular one was to place a pair of scissors, sewing shears or a knife under the doormat or on window sills. This prevented a witch entering a house or if she did her power would not work on its occupants. Outside in their gardens the country folk planted thick hedges of holly or blackthorn around their properties. These were designed not only to deter burglars but also as a psychic barrier to keep witches and evil spirits out. Writing at the end of the 18th century Thomas Chatterton said: 'Against Foul Fiends, the Holly Bush and Churchyard Yew are certain Antidotes.'

In the 16th and 17th centuries the outer walls of houses in East Anglia were also decorated with what have been described as 'ritual protection marks.' Some are said to have been put there by builders or by merchants who owned the houses originally and used them for trading. A few appear to be of pagan origin and included the Germanic runes and the ancient symbol of the sun wheel. The *dagaz* rune symbolizing dawn and the light is found on both secular buildings and churches, notably at the parish church of Aldeby in Norfolk. It is probably a spiritual legacy from the occupation of the area in the early medieval period by the Anglo-Saxons and then the Danes.

Hex signs almost identical to those found among the Pennsylvanian Dutch (*Deutch* or German immigrants) in the United States can also be found in East Anglia. One example on a Cambridgeshire church has been dated to the 14th century. Another was found on the north door of a church at Denton, Norfolk. In folklore the north door was known as the 'Devil's door.' This may date back to the early period of dual observance in the transition from paganism to Christianity. Then churches sometimes had two altars—one pagan and one Christian—and the heathens entered the church through the north door to worship the Old Gods. At the church in the Suffolk village of Stanningfield there was a glazed tile decorated with a horseshoe. This was supposed to have been placed there to keep local witches from entering the church and stealing the host. In 1795 a woman believed to be a witch was 'swam' in the pond next to the church. (John Glyde Junior 1866:31)

Horse skulls have already been mentioned and in present-day renovations of old cottages and farmhouses in East Anglia various other good luck charms and foundation sacrifices have been found. These include mummified cats and mice, silver coins, shoes and the traditional witch's besom. In his research in the 1980s into ritual deposits in houses Nigel Pennick found fifteen references to mummified cats found in houses in Cambridgeshire, Essex, Suffolk and Norfolk (2006:74–75). It was considered bad luck to move them from their hiding places and the finders were recommended to leave them alone. Pennick believes that some of the mummified cats and feline bones found in houses may be the remains of pet animals used as witches' familiars. They were interred either when they died or when their owners died and for that reason it was considered unlucky to disturb them (1995:145).

Eveline C. Gudron mentioned an old fisherman, Thomas Colson, who was a resident of St Clement near Ipswich. He was an educated man who had read widely on the subject of witchcraft and for that reason had gained a reputation as a wizard. He became convinced that he was permanently under psychic attack from witches. As protection he wore numerous charms and amulets including horse bones and animal teeth, rings with semi-precious stones set in them and scraps of parchment with magical sigils on them. Unfortunately his beliefs were his eventual undoing. One dark and stormy night the man set off fishing because he believed his charms would offer magical protection from the elemental forces of nature. When his boat was swamped by high waves Colston refused to abandon it believing it was safe and he was drowned (Gudron 1896:56–57).

The iron witch bottles made by a blacksmith and used by Cunning James Murrell have been discussed and there are many other examples of their use in East Anglian witchcraft. Several pottery examples have been found in Suffolk in recent times and they were decorated with grotesque faces and masks. One discovered in 1958 during the excavation of the new Ipswich Civic College had a horseshoe design on it. Forensic examinations of these vessel revealed they contained iron nails, bent pins, small pointed wooden sticks, human hair, nail cuttings and phosphates suggesting the presence of human urine (Wright 2004:19).

In his *Sadducismus Triumphatus* (1683) Joseph Glanvil, chaplain to King Charles II, published the story of a priest and scholar from Christ College, Cambridge who lodged at a house in Suffolk when visiting the county. The wife of his landlord was suffering from ill-health because of the frequent manifestation of a 'thing' in the shape of a large black bird that fluttered in her face. In desperation the couple consulted a traveling cunning man for his advice on how to exorcise the unwanted spirit. The cunning man recommended the landlord get a glass bottle and fill it with his wife's urine. Pins, needles and nails were added and the mouth of the bottle was sealed tight with a cork. The vessel was then placed on an open fire and boiled up until it broke. Several bottles were needed to banish the bird spirit and it led to the unexpected death of a known wizard. His wife said that before he died the man had confessed to sending the spirit to harass the couple.

Witch bottles were also used in love magic. In 1919 a Norwich witch cast a spell to bring her daughter and son-in-law back together. They had separated while the husband was away fighting in the trenches in the First World War. On his return the man, who was probably 'shell-shocked' or suffering from what we call today post-traumatic stress disorder, refused to have anything to do with his wife. The witch-mother placed some of her daughter's pubic hair, urine and nail clippings in a bottle and heated it until it burst. The following week her son-in-law called on his wife and within a month they were back together in the marital bed.

Bottles were also used to ward off the spells of witches. Filled with colored threads they were hung from the wooden roof beams of cottages so they could be seen from outside. Witch-balls, made from blue, green or red glass and about six or eight inches in diameter, were also hung in windows to avert the Evil Eye. One example preserved in the Cambridge Folk Museum is dated 1792. If the reflective surface of the ball went dull or tarnished its owner knew it had done its job. It had successfully absorbed the negative energy rays projected by a passing witch. Glass walking sticks, often containing twisted strands of colored glass, were also used to ward off the powers of witchcraft.

Glass vessels were also used by cunning folk to trap and contain spirits rather like the Middle Eastern legend of the genie in a bottle. In a manuscript written by John Saltmarsh, an academic at Kings College, Cambridge, for the Eastern Counties Folklore Society he described such a spirit vessel containing a clerical ghost. Saltmarsh described a haunting at a rectory on the Cambridgeshire and Suffolk border following the murder in a drunken fight of a vicar by his butler. In the 1870s the new recumbent and his wife were so disturbed by the ghostly happenings that they had the restless spirit exorcised by no less then eleven clergyman. They allegedly forced it into a bottle that was sealed with a cork and wax and placed in a cupboard in a wall cavity that was then plastered over. The key to the cupboard was thrown in the pond in the rectory garden.

In the 1920s a builder was employed by the then vicar to do some work at the rectory. The housekeeper told him about the ghost story and how the vicar's spirit was sealed in the bottle. The builder decided to play a practical joke on the superstitious woman. He got an old bottle and pretended he had broken into the cupboard. He showed his find to the housekeeper and opened it up. Her face went white and she fled from the room in terror with the builder's laughter ringing in her ears. The vicar was upset at the builder's joke because he said such stories should not be treated as mere superstition because however fantastic they contained some truth (*Fortean Times*, FT242, 2007).

8

The Decline in Witch Belief

BY THE LATE 17th century the number of trials for witchcraft had dramatically decreased. From the 1670s onwards few cunning men and wise women were prosecuted under the 1604 Witchcraft Act for conjuring spirits (Davies 2003:20). Although this reflected a more progressive and liberalized legal system popular and hostile attitudes towards the power of witchcraft persisted. Some of the clergy adopted an enlightened and skeptical approach to the subject, while others took the opposite view. Many backward-looking churchmen saw witchcraft as a real and serious crime that should still be punished by the law. In fact it was an evil that had to be combated at every possible opportunity.

In 1693 the Reverend Samuel Potts of Sudbury in Suffolk published his account of the 'wonderful and extraordinary fits' suffered by a local man Thomas Spatchett allegedly due to the practice of witchcraft. The person believed to be responsible was identified and when she was questioned by the minister confessed. However when the case came to court the magistrates would not accept her confession as reliable evidence. A disappointed Reverend Potts noted critically that 'notwithstanding what could be witnessed against her, yet she was sent home; and nothing in point of law was done against her.' He had wanted her punished with a lengthy prison sentence for her alleged crime (Gudron 1896:35).

The next year Margaret Elinore from Ipswich was charged with inflicting an illness on a woman who refused to rent her some property. As soon as the alleged witch was imprisoned the victim recovered. After searching Elinore the authorities claimed to have found extra nipples on her body they claimed were used to feed her imps. Witnesses testified that the witch had learnt the art and inherited her nine imps from her relatives. In fact both her grandmother and mother had been hanged as witches. Fortunately for Margaret Elinore her case was heard by a liberal judge, John Holt. He rejected the witness statements and ordered her to be released.

Justice John Holt also presided over the trial of a Bury St Edmund's witch who was supposed to have cursed her landlord when he evicted her. He died shortly afterwards and the gossips said she was responsible. They claimed the woman had killed her landlord with witchcraft and had a familiar spirit in the shape of a domesticated polecat. One prominent witness strangely was a doctor who described the alleged witch as a 'dangerous woman' who could 'touch the line of life.' Again the judge was not convinced by the evidence provided by the witnesses, despite the doctor's credibility and social standing in the community, and all the charges were dropped.

In 1715 Richard Boulton published his *Complete History of Magic, Sorcery and Witchcraft* and in it he explained his personal belief in the power of witchcraft, the existence of familiar spirits and that witches flew through the air on broomsticks and made pacts with the Devil. His old-fashioned and unenlightened views were attacked by an elderly clergyman the Reverend Francis Hutchinson, who had been a young minister at Bury St Edmunds during the time of the witch trials. In his own treatise *A Historical Essay Concerning Witchcraft*, published in 1718, the Reverend Hutchinson condemned accusations of witchcraft based solely on the evidence of perjurers, small children and the delusions of sick minds. Controversially the clergyman also criticized the political factors he claimed often influenced the authorities in their decisions to prosecute alleged witches.

The tide was turning but as James Sharpe has said: '...the decline of witchcraft beliefs in post-Restoration England [after King Charles II was crowned in 1660] cannot be interpreted as any simple triumph of reason over superstition or science over theology' (1996:244). While learned opinion was becoming more skeptical about the actual power of witchcraft the popular belief in it still survived. This belief took the traditional form that had been known in the witch trials. For instance in 1716 a woman and her nine-year-old daughter in Huntingdon were believed to have sold their souls to the Devil. The mother was also accused of raising storms merely by washing her dirty stockings in a wooden bucket (Newman 1946:21).

In 1735, just before the old Witchcraft Act of 1604 was repealed, the *Ipswich Gazette* reported that a man had been 'swam' as a suspected witch. John Kiniman from Kelmarsh was dragged to the village pond by an angry mob and placed in the ducking stool normally used for punishing scolds and gossips. His attackers claimed Kiniman had conspired with his dark master the Devil to cast spells to ruin the butter and cheese made by the local dairywomen.

The parish register at Monk's Eleigh in Suffolk for December 19th 1748 recorded that a laborer's wife, Alice Green, was 'swam' as a witch. This happened because 'certain evil and malicious people' had spread rumors she was a witch (*The East Anglian* magazine, Volume 1, 1848:48) Four years later some people 'full of ignorance and superstition' seized and tied up several elderly people they thought were witches and wizards. They then threw them into a river to see if they floated or sank. The death of cattle from disease and the failure of crops were blamed on the activities of these alleged witches. (*The Norwich Gazette*, September 1752). Their ultimate fate is not recorded but hopefully they were rescued from their persecutors by more sensible people.

In June 1792 a woman from Stanningfield (Suffolk) allowed herself to be examined by a local tribunal made up of two magistrates, the vicar and the squire. This was to clear her name from an accusation of practicing witchcraft. The woman also asked to be weighed against the church Bible to prove her innocence. When the clergyman refused her request as a 'base superstition' the desperate woman volunteered to be 'swum.' This took place unofficially in the village pond with incredibly her husband and brother presiding over the event. The woman could not swim and she sank to the bottom of the pond. She was dragged out of the water 'almost lifeless' (Gursdon 1893:185).

In 1825 Isaac Stebbings of Wickham (Suffolk) was believed to have bewitched two women. When an anti-witchcraft ritual was being performed at the house of one of the victims Stebbings coincidently knocked on the door. This was enough for him to be accused, although he insisted his visit was quite innocent. He was selling mackerel door to door, even though it was only 4 a.m. in the morning. Stebbings volunteered for the 'swimming' test to clear his name. Unfortunately he floated and in the eyes of his accusers that confirmed his guilt. A second 'swimming' was planned until the vicar intervened and forbade any of his parishioners to take part (Hole 1977: 172–173).

Thirty-seven years later at Headingham, Essex an elderly deaf mute of French birth known by the unfortunate nickname 'Dummy' was 'swam' for bewitching a local girl. He looked like a scarecrow and lived in a hut at the edge of the village eking out a meager living as a cunning man. The disabled Frenchmen told fortunes, practised love spells and found missing or stolen property. A young woman called Emma Smith accused Dummy of putting a spell on her. She hit him with a stick and, with a male friend and forty other people cheering them on, pushed the disabled man into a stream. He was taken to the workhouse and died from pneumonia as the result of his ordeal. Smith and her friend were each sentenced to six months in jail for assault.

In the early 1800s an old woman at Monk Solom in Suffolk was thrown into a pit by a mob and was killed. It was claimed she must have been a witch purely because she had a black cat as a pet and always wore a black silk dress when attending church services even if it was not a funeral. The villagers speculated how she could afford such an expensive dress. They decided that the woman could have only gotten it through practicing the art of witchcraft as it was well known she was as poor as the proverbial church mouse. It must have been given to her by the Devil because it was well known he supplied his devotees with material goods if they sold their souls to him.

'Old Judy', the so-called Witch of Burrell in the Cambridgeshire fens, lived in a traditional one-storey cottage built of wattle-and-daub (hazel sticks and mud) with a sedge and rush thatch roof. Locals described her as 'a wicked old crone...with a high crowned black hat and a black tom-cat, whose looks were as bad as her deeds' (Porter 1962:162). This is an archetypical, if not stereotypical, description of the popular image of a witch as an old woman, usually either an 'old maid' (spinster) or a widow, living alone with her pet cat as her only companion.

One famous witch Elizabeth Fyson (1723–1804) was popularly known in later years by the seemingly respectable title of Old Mother Fyson. For a small fee she would predict the sex of unborn babies and also did healing and found lost property. However, like so many of the so-called 'white witches', she had a darker side. For a much larger fee Fyson would concoct a potion to get rid of unwanted or unfaithful husbands and lovers. A story is told of a couple consulting her and one asked the other; 'I wonder if the old witch is home?' When they reached her house Old Mother Fyson was standing on the doorstep waiting for them and said: 'Come in my dears, the old witch is here' (*Notes and Queries*, 1858:457).

In the 1850s a renowned witch called Goody Gardner lived at Thorpe-le-Stoken in Suffolk. When she was supposed to have bewitched a flock of geese belonging to a smallholder he burnt one of the dead ones to break the spell. Almost immediately the neighbors heard terrible screaming coming from Goody Gardner's cottage. She was seen running from the building with her clothes and hair on fire. She died in agony some time later and her body was covered all over with burns.

At Norton also in Suffolk in 1855 an elderly woman called Mrs Osborn was reputed to be a hereditary witch who had gotten her powers from her mother's side of the family. She made a living as a fortune-teller and one of her clients said Osborn predicted she would marry a man who used a large hammer in his daily work. Shortly afterwards she met and married a blacksmith. Unfortunately someone claimed that after Osborn had visited the house to give a consultation the family's pig fell ill. Its owner blamed the witch and to counter her spell snipped off a small piece of the animals' tail. She threw it in the fire and the pig recovered (Wright 2004:44).

Another famed Cambridgeshire witch was Susan Cooper (1810–1880). It was said she went to visit a house and could not gain access as its owner had placed a pair of scissors under the doormat. On another occasion the householder placed an iron knife under a cushion on a chair. When Cooper sat down she immediately jumped up saying: 'You've hidden a knife under ther'!'

In 1856 the *Bury and Norwich Post* reported the apprehension of a burglar at Breckland in Suffolk. Three men had been seen acting suspiciously near a house and the owner chased them off. He caught up with one of the men and hit him over the head with a piece of wood. The would-be burglar was arrested and when he appeared in court he was identified as wanted man called Tom Gathercote. The police were already seeking him in connection with a number of robberies in the area. It was said that Gathercote evaded capture because his late mother was a witch. Before she died she gave her son a magical charm that allowed to him escape justice. Apparently after her death it ceased to be effective and he was caught and imprisoned.

A year later a Norfolk schoolmaster asked his class to define the meaning of the word 'witch.' In their replies all the children referenced somebody they knew who was supposed to be one (*The Times*, April 27th 1857). In the same year a farmer from Hockham in Norfolk told a magistrate that witchcraft was on the increase: 'They do say, your worship, that such folks [witches] are increased about in the world, and if you have so many as even one in this or any other parish, they do a sight of harm.' The farmer had appeared in court to ask for a restraining order on a local woman he thought had 'witched' his wife 'good and proper like.' He even asked the magistrate to order the police to 'swim' the suspected witch. Naturally this request was turned down (*The Times*, April 7th 1857).

In another case brought before the magistrates in Norwich in 1859 a woman applied for a restraining order on her own forty year-old son. The mother said that she believed he had placed a spell on her. The man protested that he was innocent and that a cunning man his mother had consulted had put the idea in her head. Despite this spirited defense the magistrate ordered the son to leave his parent's home and pay the legal costs of the case. When the man said he had no money he was jailed (Davies 2003:203–204).

When in 1863 the future King Edward VII, then the Prince of Wales, bought Sandringham in Norfolk as a royal holiday home he evicted several tenants from the estate. However one was allowed to stay as she was renowned as a 'wise woman' and the estate's agent was too frightened to get rid of her. She was widely respected and consulted as a herbalist and healer and in 1880 when the prince fell ill his servants secretly contacted her. The wise woman recommended some of her mandrake wine should be drunk by the prince and, whether it worked or not, the future king soon recovered.

At the seaside town of Great Yarmouth on the Norfolk coast a woman took her son to a cunning woman called Mrs Mortimer because she believed he had eaten some bewitched sausages. After a sovereign was handed over the mother was told to look into a 'divining cup' to see who was responsible but refused as she was too scared. Instead Mrs Mortimer gave the sick man a copy of the Lord's Prayer to wear 'near your heart' and a herbal potion to drink. She also asked for a lock of hair, some of his nail parings and a small bottle of urine so she could 'work on them' if the paper and the potion did not work. The man recovered and Mrs Mortimer asked for a further ten shillings for her services. When this was not forthcoming the man became ill again and was forced to pay the cunning woman in order to recover (Glyde 1872:57–58).

At Hockley in the 1880s anyone who dared to cross the resident witch, Nelly Button, was in danger of losing the use of their limbs. In one case a girl she had cursed had been unable to move for a week and had to stay in bed. Button decided to lift the spell and walked into the kitchen where the girl was sitting. She whispered some unknown words in her ear. Within five minutes the girl had recovered the full use of her legs and was gaily skipping around the room.

One day the village blacksmith argued with Nelly Button. In revenge she made his prized concertina play all night on its own. Whatever the smith did he could not make it stop and had to destroy it. She punished a woman she fell out with by making the dumplings she was cooking fly out of the saucepan on to the ceiling, walls and floor. Eventually the villagers trapped the witch in her home by circling it with knives and scissors. They knew this would negate her magical powers and stop her doing any further harm to people (Maple 1962:183).

In 1890 an inquest was held that illustrated the superstitious fear of witches and their powers was held at Fressingfield in Suffolk. The hearing concerned the mysterious death of a ten-week-old baby, Emma Hammond, whose parents were convinced she had been bewitched to death. The person responsible was supposed to have been the child's hated step-grandmother, Mrs Corbyn. She had died a few hours previous to the baby predicting with her last breath it would soon follow her. The infant was taken out for a walk in a pram and wisps of smoke were seen coming from inside the vehicle. On checking the baby was found dead. A medical examination revealed that it had died from the 'external application of an unknown irritant.' George Corbyn, the baby's grandfather, told the inquest he had always believed his dead wife had the powers of a witch. For that reason he always did what she wanted (Wright 2004:3).

At the end of the 19th and the beginning of the 20th century the Essex village of Canewdon, the last home of Old George Pickingill, was well known for its many witches, black and white and gray. The first record instance of witchcraft in the village was that of Rose Pye in the late 16th century. She was said to have bewitched to death the newborn baby of a local tailor called Richard Snowe who lived at Scaldhurst Farm. Pye appeared at the Chelmsford assizes in 1576 and pleaded not guilty. However she failed to come to trial because she died while waiting in prison. Nine years later Cicely Malkin (a surname that oddly is a rural nickname for a hare) was accused of practicing witchcraft. She agreed to confess to the crime and do a public penance in the parish church. In 1590 she was actually excommunicated for some unknown reason, a rare penalty for what was widely regarded as the worst of crimes.

As mentioned earlier when George Pickingill was discussed, amateur folklorist and Gas Board engineer Eric Maple visited the Southend area in Essex in 1959 to recuperate from a chest infection. While he was there he collected numerous stories and anecdotes from elderly local people. Among the witch legends about Canewdon he collected was that were as 'many witches in silk as in cotton' in the village. Also while the bell tower of St Nicholas church remains standing there will always be six witches in Canewdon. One will be the vicar's wife, one the butcher's wife and another the baker's wife. Every time a stone falls from the tower it was believed a witch died and had to be replaced.

In the 1840s, when Cunning Murrell was visiting Canewdon, the folklore about witches in silk and cotton was said to be proved by the fact that the vicar's wife, Mary Ann Atkinson, was the sister of Lady Lodwick who owned considerable land in the village. She was in fact Eliza Frost Kersteman and the family was descended from Flemish settlers who came to East Anglia in the 1700s to work in the weaving trade. In an interview with *The Times* in the late 1950s a local resident, an elderly man called Arthur Downes, said when he was a child he was told that two of the witches of Canewdon had been 'the passon's [parson] wife' and 'Owd Lady Lodwick.' When her husband died in 1857 Mary Ann Kersteman-Atkinson moved in with her alleged witch-sister at the family home of Lambourne Hall in Canewdon.

When Eric Maple visited Canewdon in the late 1950s and early 1960s elderly inhabitants told him the initials of the six witches living in the village sixty years earlier at the turn of the century. They were Mrs W, a cripple; Mrs K, who lived 'by the churchyard', Mrs L.A., Mrs M., Mrs C. and Mrs L. Local historian and Canewdon resident Sibyl M. Webster identified four of these named women as Mrs Whybrow, who was disabled, Mrs Killworth, whose cottage was in the lane leading up to the church not far from where Lillian Garner's family lived, and who was reputed to be a witch, Mrs Maskell, who belonged to a family long associated with the practice of witchcraft; and Mrs Lanham who lived at Rest Cottages and was well known as a healer and wart-charmer (Webster 2005:172). In the 1960s Rest Cottages was the home of a reputed male witch called Bibby Kemp, possibly a relation of the famous

16th century St Osyth witch Ursula Kemp. When a General Post Office linesman upset him one day the old man cursed him. The next day the engineer fell from a telegraph pole he was working on and was very badly injured.

Traditionally the animal associated with the familiars of the Canewdon witches were white rabbits or white mice. In fact even in the 1960s if the village darts team failed to score or lost a match they would mutter 'White mice!' and blame the local witches for their bad luck (ibid:171). In the 1890s an old woman lived at the smithy and one day she was visited by her granddaughter. The girl had always been frightened by her elderly relative and for that reason tried not to be alone with her. This particular day she could not avoid it and was in dread of what might happen to her. The grandmother turned to the girl and giving a hideous laugh pulled a small bag from her blouse. It was heaving and squirming as if it contained a nest of mice. The old woman told the terrified girl that it contained her imps. That night the grandmother appeared at her bedside. Her mother consulted a wise woman and a witch bottle was prepared. As it boiled there was a loud scratching at the door. When the girl cried out in terror it stopped. The next day the grandmother was found dead in her bed. (Maple 1962:186–187). It is possible that by showing the girl her imps she was trying to pass on her 'virtue' or power to her granddaughter through her familiars.

In 1889 Henry Laver wrote an article giving his own personal recollections of meeting one of the famous witches from Canewdon called Old Mother Cowling. In his opinion she was 'an old harmless woman… who was credited with the possession of fearful powers' by the superstitious villagers (Fifty Years Ago in Essex, *The Essex Naturalist* III, January–June 1889). This indicated that as well as a fear of witches and witchcraft among the rural population at this time the more educated intelligentsia were skeptical about such surviving and persisting beliefs in country districts.

In the early 1900s, the Edwardian period that followed after the death of Queen Victoria in 1901, St Stephen's Back Street in Norwich was known as 'a sort of Harley Street for white witches.' Harley Street was in London and was famous for its surgeries and clinics owned by private doctors, surgeons and psychiatrists. The 'white witches' in Norwich were eagerly consulted by the country folk who came into the city to attend the weekly livestock markets and the annual fair (*Eastern Daily News*, December 18th 1968).

In the same period however the Reverend Charles Kent, the rector of Merton in Norfolk, expressed his personal belief in the power of witchcraft with a surprisingly modern attitude: 'My own belief in witchery, as they term it about here, is possibly not so crude as that of some of my older parishioners. I believe in the power of hate so working on the power of faith that evil results. Witchery is hate made manifest' (Summers 1927:182). Writing about the 'child-like' faith in the supernatural by East Anglian people, folklorist Emily Frances Cranworth said such beliefs were usually held in private. Publicly, and especially to outsiders, they were ashamed to admit they believed in the power of witchcraft (*Eastern Counties Magazine*, 1900).

A local newspaper at Bottisham near Cambridge reported in 1904 that this belief in the supernatural, ghosts and witches still persisted. A twenty-seven-year-old timber merchant was imprisoned for cruelty to his three horses. The court heard that he had believed they had been bewitched by an enemy or rival. To try and break the spell he fed them a broth he had cooked up by boiling a pennyworth of pins and some pieces of horse's hoof over an open fire. He had drained the liquid off and gave it to the animals. It was not said how he knew this method of countering a spell but it must have been fairly common knowledge.

At the annual Dunmow Flower Show in Essex in 1920 several exhibitors who had previously won prizes complained to the organizers that their blooms had been attacked and destroyed by birds. Only one member's flowers were left untouched and naturally he walked away with all the medals. Witchcraft was suspected and there was a lot of muttering and the pointing of fingers. People noted that the prize-winner was a professional fortune-teller, which was regarded as a suspicious line of work under the circumstances. It was even said the man had a strange power over animals. When he whistled wild birds flew to him and ate out of his hand (Morgan 1982:130). As seen earlier have seen power over animals and birds was one of the powers credited to cunning men and women.

In an article in *The Times* in September 1930 about the survival of witchcraft in Essex, E.K. Venner said: 'Belief in witches is always very cautiously admitted and generally indirectly, so some care is necessary to catch it when it comes to the surface.' In the same article Venner, probably jokingly, asked an Essex woman if she had ever seen the local witch flying on a broomstick. He got the incredible reply that she had never seen such a sight 'but then you see she be right at the end of the [village] green.'

In 1947 Gordon Sutton of East Dereham, Norfolk appeared in the magistrate's court for assaulting his neighbor, Mrs Spinks. Defending his action, Sutton said he had been forced to attack the victim to make her go away. She had, he claimed, made his life a misery for the last five years with 'her witchcraft.' The woman had repeatedly tied bunches of wild flowers to his garden gate. Every time he had spat on them and thrown them away. Mrs Spinks denied being a witch and said the trouble had started when Sutton accused her of picking the herb parsley from his garden without his permission. Both Sutton and Mrs Spinks were told to behave themselves in future and were bound over by the court to keep the peace (Porter 1974:160).

Until 1953 when its ruins were swept away in the Great Flood that engulfed parts of East Anglia that year, a large brick built house on Wallasea Island on the River Crouch near Canewdon was known as Duval's House or Devil House Farm. It had been seriously damaged by a German Luftwaffe in the Second World War when it was hit by a bomb and the flood waters swept the ruins away. It was once the home of an elderly woman called Mrs Smith, who was more commonly known locally by the generic witch name 'Old Mother Redcap.' A farm laborer who worked for many years on Wallasea Island said that when she was seeding potatoes the witch would sing out: 'Holly, Brolly, Redcap, Bonny' (Pennick 2006:110). These were supposed to be the names of her familiar spirits and she was probably evoking them to help supply a good crop.

Both Old Mother Redcap's ghost and her familiars were supposed to have haunted the house after she died. Visitors mentioned psychic 'cold spots' in the house associated with paranormal manifestations. The sound of great wings, as if they belonged to some kind of giant bird, where heard flapping in one room. Other people reported seeing phantom white mice scampering around the house and even the horrifying apparition of a small and hideous looking ape-like creature. For these reasons most local people shunned the Devil's House after dark (Maple, Autumn 1965).

In the early 1960s two journalists on a local Essex newspaper, the late Peter Haining and his colleague A.V. Sellwood, conducted an investigation into witchcraft and Satanism. The result of their research was published in a sensational paperback book *Devil Worship in Britain*

(1964). Haining later wrote more serious books on historical witchcraft and edited anthologies of classic horror stories. The investigation began when he wrote an article on the occult for the newspaper mentioning Essex's long historical connection with witchcraft. As a result Haining received a letter from a village in the remote Rodings area from somebody using the pseudonym 'Vigilant'. The writer said that not only was witchcraft of a historical type still flourishing in modern Essex but he could prove it to the journalists.

Subsequently the two occult investigators met the letter writer in a café in Leigh-on-Sea. They described him as quite normal and a 'neatly-dressed and unobtrusively mannered engineer.' Their contact told them that there was a 'black witchcraft' coven operating only a few miles from where they were sitting. If the two men were interested he could take them to its meeting place when the group next gathered to do a ritual. The man said he was not a member of the coven, but he seemed to have inside knowledge of its activities.

A fortnight later the two journalists were led by their informant to a hiding place in the bracken in a wood overlooking a hollow. The hollow was a shallow bowl in the ground forming a natural circle of moss, short grass and toadstools. At midnight in the misty autumn moonlight they watched as eleven robed and hooded figures entered it. They were led by a tall elderly man wearing a short black cloak over his robe decorated with a gold pentagram or five-pointed star. The person walking behind him carried a censer on a chain that they swung from side to side emitting a cloud of fragrant incense. Other members of the coven followed carrying a small wooden table, a slab of stone and two cloths.

Quickly and efficiently as if they had done it many times, the members of the coven carried out their obviously allocated tasks. The table was set up with a heavily embroidered cloth thrown over it to form an improvised altar. The stone slab was placed on the ground next to it and covered with the second cloth that was marked with occult sigils. A silver chalice and other objects were placed on the altar and a small fire was lit in the circle. Finally a number of gold symbols were hung in the lowest branches of the surrounding trees. The journalists were told by their informant that this was to form a protective psychic barrier to keep out any intruders.

The rite began with the high priest or witch-master chanting mournfully in Latin and slowly raising his arms to the sky. The others joined in and the concealed watchers could smell the clogging sweetness of the incense as more was burnt in the censer. One of the five women present undid her robe and dropped it to the ground. Underneath she wore a short, tight fitting, one-piece tunic-type dress with a deep neckline revealing her breasts. The journalists were later told by their informant she was the 'witch-maiden' or female leader of the coven. Apparently she had the 'witch name' of Tanith, an ancient Phoenician moon goddess of fertility worshipped in North Africa. The purpose of this evening's rite was necromancy and the coven was attempting to communicate with the spirits of the dead.

The witch-master handed Tanith two large masks with grotesque features and she placed them on the altar on either side of the chalice. The informant told the journalists these were used when the spirits manifested. Wine was poured into the vessel and it was passed around the circle for everyone to take a drink from. Another chant started up, which the journalists identified as 'the original witch language' (possibly Anglo-Saxon or Old English). The young woman moved in front of the witch-master and he stared into her eyes for nearly a minute. Then she was lifted up by two men on to the altar where she lay prone and still as if unconscious.

The celebrant of the rite then took a medieval-type sword from under his cloak and used it to trace a circle on the ground around the fire. He then made a series of ritual genuflections towards the altar. The other coven members turned towards the four points of the compass in sequence. They then removed their robes and danced naked wildly around the altar and the prone witch-maiden on it. As they danced in frenzy the witch-master threw some powder into the flames of the fire and swirling clouds of white smoke and sparks rose into the night sky. Then the witch-maiden raised herself up from the altar. Her body was rigid 'like a wooden doll' and she spoke in a low voice that the concealed witnesses could not hear. The witch-master listened intently to what she had to say. After a few minutes of speaking she fell back on the altar.

That seemed to be the conclusion of the rite and the dancers slumped to the ground exhausted. More wine was passed around in the chalice, but this time it seemed to be drunk for refreshment rather than any ritualistic purpose as it was before. The young woman, now out of her trance, was helped off the altar by her two guardians. Everyone robed up again and the circle was cleared of the altar and all the other objects. The fire was dowsed and made safe. The coven then left the hollow in a single file procession using the woodland path they had come in by.

Two hours had passed since the rite had begun (A.V. Sellwood and Peter Haining 1964:81–88).

Afterwards journalists were told by their anonymous informant that the ritual they had witnessed in the Essex countryside was an example of 'black magic' carried out by devil-worshippers. Because of their own agenda Haining and Sellwood were quite happy to believe what he said. However its necromantic nature and the closeness of the ritual to Hallowe'en suggest it was an attempt by a traditional coven to contact and channel the spirits of the dead through its maiden or high priestess. It is possible that the informant had a reason to blacken the name of the coven and he may possibly have been a disgruntled ex-member. This would explain why he knew about their meeting place and the date and time of the ritual.

In 1963 and 1964 a series of what the newspapers 'black magic rites' were performed across southern England in the Home Counties of Bedfordshire, Sussex and Kent involving the desecration of churches and graves. One of these in December 1963 was at St Clements church at Leigh-on-Sea. As at Castle Rising a few months earlier, it featured a traditional counter-witchcraft charm of a sheep's heart pierced with thirteen hawthorns. The magical object had been placed on top of a tomb and was framed with a letter 'A' made from small stones or grave chippings. This was possibly the initial of the person's name the magical working was directed against. Unlike the Norfolk churches, St Clements was not ruined and unconsecrated and was in daily use for services.

At Hallowe'en 1975 villagers living near some woods in Essex called The Scrubs heard blood-curdling screams and saw lights flickering in the trees. Next day in an isolated clearing they found a twenty-foot circle made of branches. Inside it was a twelve-inch toy doll fixed to a branch with a metal spike. Six hatpins had also been driven into vital parts of the poppet's body. The image was covered in red candle wax and next to it were the remains of a partly burnt black candle. Nearby several twigs had been arranged on the ground to form a pentagram and the same occult symbol was chalked on the trees surrounding the circle ('Curse of the Doll of Death', Eric Maple, *Weekend* magazine, October 1977).

Canewdon's historical reputation as a 'witch village' has survived into modern times. There used to be a life sized carved image of a black cat at St Nicholas' church. It was a fierce and scary looking feline and according to the vicar had started life as a medieval gargoyle in a West

Country church. Some years ago it was stolen from its resting place and was never seen again. Local rumor suggested the image had been taken by the thieves for use in some kind of 'black witchcraft' ritual (Morgan 1973:62).

When plans were drawn up in the 1970s to extend the international airport at Stansted in Essex many of the villages that were to be affected by the building work or flight paths formed protest groups. One of them was Canewdon and a local councilor told the *London Evening Standard* newspaper he believed the witches who still lived in the village would be working spells in the traditional way to stop the development going ahead. Today the churchyard at St Nicholas has CCTV cameras installed to deter witchcraft associated vandalism. Every Hallowe'en the police have to control carloads of curious people who turn up in the village 'looking for the witches.'

In recent years evidence of so-called 'satanic rites' have been discovered at the ruined church of St Mary at Houghton-on-the-Hill near Swaffham (Suffolk). Built on the ancient site of an early Saxon chapel, the present medieval church lay in ruins in thick woods for many years. It was rediscovered during a Women's Institute outing and has now been fully renovated. The church roof had collapsed, the crumbling walls were covered in ivy, and the churchyard was totally overgrown with tall weeds and shrubs hiding the graves from view.

The renovators of St Mary's found that persons unknown had been using the ruined church as an alleged 'satanic temple.' There were signs of regular fires being lit in the nave and stone crosses had been turned upside down. Some of the graves outside had been desecrated and a tomb had been pried open using a wooden stake. A human skull and some bones had been taken from inside it and used in a ritual. Today the 'church in the woods' has been reconsecrated. It has hundreds of visitors and at least once a year a service is held in its precincts.

E.W. Liddell, who now lives in Australia and claims to be a hereditary member of the Pickingill witch family, has described how traditional witchcraft is still practised in modern East Anglia. In the initiation ceremony into the witch-cult a male witch sexually inducts a female candidate and vice-versa. The site of the ritual has to be a prehistoric burial mound, a place where a suicide has taken place or an ancient battle fought, a churchyard or a crossroads. In fact any place associated with death where the initiate can make psychic contact with their spirit guides and the ancestral dead. A small bird or animal is sacrificed to the witch-god in his aspect as the Lord of Death (e.g., Woden) and to the *genii loci* or the 'spirits of place', the wights or earth spirits. The sacrifice is then buried in the ground to 'feed the land' (Letter from E.W. Liddell to Dr Ronald Hutton, Professor of History at the University of Bristol, England, August 11th 1998).

Another modern Essex cunning man and traditional witch, the late Andrew D. Chumbley has described his own native witchcraft tradition. Writing in 1993 he said that majority of Essex witches were and are solitary practitioners specializing in wort-cunning, mediumship or enchantment, although they come together periodically to practice their Art. Their practices as in the old days include curing and cursing and rituals, spells and magical formulae, often employed in the idiom of the predominant religious culture of Christianity. However Essex witchcraft also employs the ancient methodology and tools of magic such as the ritual circle, the wand, knife, cord, knot, and charm, plus stellar lore, local flora and fauna, spirit evocation and invocation and exorcism. It also includes the mythos of the Wild Hunt and the Witches Sabbath as 'an astral or dream convocation of the souls of the witches, animal selves, spirits, faeries, and familiars.' ('The Sabazean Torch', *The Occult Observer* magazine, Volume II, 4, 1993 and 'Cultus Sabbati: Provenance, Dream and Magistry' www.xoanon.co.uk) One of Chumbley's contacts into the Old Craft, and the elder of his initiatory lineage, had been inducted by a rural circle of wise women in Buckinghamshire in the 1940s, but lived in Essex and belonged to at least one traditional 'old' coven in the county.

9

Black Shuck, Pharisees and Hikey Sprites

THE NORFOLK POACHER mentioned earlier in relation to the toad bone ritual said: 'The Younger Generation do not believe a lot that the old ones tell them these days. There used to be all sorts of legends in those days, ghosts of all sorts, tales of Weanling Calves and shaggy Dogs that walked on the high way, and men ridden about with no Heads on, and Panthom Carriage running about the Cuntry side, I never see none of them but the Old People believed it was all true' (edited by Rider Haggard 1935:15 with original spelling).

The 'shaggy Dogs' mentioned above was a reference to the phantom dog known in East Anglia as Black Shuck, Old Shuck, Old Shock, Shuggy and Old Scefe. These names are derived from the Old English *scucca* and the Medieval English *schucke* or 'demon' and the local East Anglian dialect 'shucky', meaning hairy or shaggy. In Suffolk the spectral Black Dog was known as Scarfe and the Galleytrot. According to *Harper's Magazine* in October 1893 in East Anglia '...young children fly terror-stricken along the roads at night fearful of meeting Shuck...' Andrew D. Chumbley mentioned in the previous chapter told this writer that when he was a schoolboy he had seen the Black Dog cross the road in front of him. In his case he did not 'fly terror-stricken.' In fact later in life Chumbley interpreted as a sign or omen of becoming a traditional magical practitioner.

The phantom Black Dog was found all over the British Isles and in general was a psychic manifestation that was regarded as demonic, associated with the Devil and an omen of death. It was often seen near places connected with death such as crossroads where gallows or gibbets stood, prehistoric burial mounds and churchyards, and also near ancient trackways. Modern Earth Mysteries researchers have connected the sightings of Black Dogs with leys or spirit paths and so-called 'death roads' or 'corpse ways', the medieval tracks used to take coffins for burial. Writing in the *Norfolk Chronicle and Norwich Gazette* in June 1805 the Reverend E.S. Taylor described Old Shuck as a 'dog fiend' that 'visits churchyards at midnight.'

Old Shucky was usually described as a large black dog about the size of a calf or a small pony with a rough shaggy coat, saucer-like eyes that glowed red or one Cyclopean eye in its forehead and large paws. Its footfalls were silent and it was said to emit a blood-chilling howl. An encounter with Shuck was regarded as bad luck and a warning that the witness would be dead before the year ended. Only rarely was it regarded as benevolent, although there are a few cases of the spectral beast protecting travelers from highwaymen or guiding them home when lost. After the encounter the phantom dog vanished by either sinking down into the earth, fading away into nothingness or dramatically disappearing in a flash of light or with a small explosion and a cloud of smoke smelling of sulphur. One man who had seen the Black Dog vanish in this way brought his neighbors to see the site, which was marked on the ground by a blackened spot as if gunpowder had been exploded on it (Glyde 1872:66).

Although some folklorists have claimed it has a Viking origin, the earliest recorded account of a Black Dog in East Anglia was at Bungay in 1577. Bungay was a prosperous town on the Suffolk and Norfolk border whose name comes from the Saxon *Bunincga-haye* or 'the land of the Bonna clan.' Before the Saxons arrived from what is now modern Germany there was a settlement at Bungay dating from Roman times. The old Stane Street, a major Roman road and military route, ran through the town leading to the modern city of Norwich. Although the Romans are always credited with building long straight roads, in many cases their surveyors were merely following the existing routes of the prehistoric trackways from the Neolithic and Bronze Ages.

On Sunday, August 4th 1577 Bungay experienced a severe thunderstorm with 'darkness, rain, hail, thunder and lightning as was never seen the like.' At the height of the storm a service was being held in the parish church of St Mary's when it was struck by lightning. There was considerable structural damage and two people attending the service, a man and a boy, were killed. Contemporary accounts say that as the storm raged the Devil appeared in the church in the form of a huge black dog accompanied by flashes of fire. The creature ran up and down the nave and passed between two kneeling members of the congregation who died on the spot. It also caused the clerk of the church, who was attempting to clear the gutter to take the water pouring off the roof, to fall off his ladder, although he was not seriously hurt. When the devil dog left the church the burn marks of its claws remained on the door.

On the same morning at nearby Blighburgh a thunderbolt struck the tower of the church causing the spire to crash through the roof into the nave. The congregation later claimed that a 'fiery demon' in the shape of a black dog entered the church by smashing open the main doors. People were knocked over and burnt as the entity, which was probably the natural phenomena known as ball lightning, rushed through the church from one end to the other. Two men and a child were also killed when they came into contact with the supposed 'fire demon.'

In the 19th century the aristocratic occupants of Blickley Hall in Norfolk were haunted by a Black Dog. It appeared after a partition wall in the mansion was demolished during building work. The phantom canine appeared every night and was also seen outside in the ground roaming in circles around the house. The owners of the house hired a 'wise man' from London to exorcise the spectral beast. He recommended that the family erect straight wooden partitions across the circle the Black Dog created when it manifested. This worked as the haunting ceased, but the cunning man said if the partitions were ever removed the apparition would return (Pennick 1995:152).

In southern and south-west England the smuggling gangs in the 18th and 19th centuries often used local folk traditions such as ghosts, phantom coaches drawn by headless horses and the Wild Hunt to conceal their nocturnal activities. Norfolk smugglers made use of the Old Shuck legend and in one case a gang tied a lantern around the neck of a black ram. They then released the animal into the fields near to the coast on nights when they were bringing their contraband ashore. In the darkness superstitious people believed it was Old Shuck and avoided the area (Platt 1991:171) At Hadleigh in Essex two ghosts known as the White Lady and the Black Man were frequently seen near the village.

However in this case more intelligent people worked out that these spectral sightings coincided with the nights local smugglers brought in their cargoes of brandy from France.

As stated above, Black Shuck was often regarded as an omen of doom and death. At Rattesden (Suffolk) a man encountered what he described as 'a thing' with saucer-like eyes. As he watched in horror the creature got bigger and bigger and he heard a gruff voice speak his name saying: 'I shall want you within the week'. The next day the man suddenly died (*East Anglian Miscellany* 1901). At Boham two men returning home from work passed the gates of Boham Hall, the stately home in the village. They were attacked by a large black dog with a long shaggy coat that ran out of the driveway. When one of the men hit it with his walking stick it went straight through its body. The creature then vanished into thin air leaving a horrible odor of sulphur behind.

In April 1901 Bertram Fletcher Robinson, a friend of Sir Arthur Conan Doyle, creator of the world famous private detective 'Sherlock Holmes', dined with the author Max Pemberton at his house in Hampstead, north-west London. Over dinner Pemberton told his guest of the spectral hound known as Black Shuck that haunted the Norfolk coastline. He claimed it had been seen recently ascending the cliff path from the beach at Cromer and loping past the Royal Links Hotel and the old Cromer Hall. Pemberton said he had been told by an old marshman that he seen the 'devil dog' at St Olives near Great Yarmouth. He described it as 'a great black hound' with 'eyes like railway lamps' When the creature crossed his path the man's own dog went mad with fear (Pugh, Spiring and Bhanji 2010:45). Conan Doyle later used the East Anglian legend of the phantom black dog in his Sherlock Holmes' story *The Hound of the Baskervilles*. Conan Doyle had also encountered local stories of sightings of the creature on Dartmoor while he was practicing as a doctor in Plymouth, Devon.

Jennifer Westwood, a member of the Folklore Society, recounted a story told in the 1940s by a Mr E. Ramsey of Bawburgh in Norfolk of a close encounter with a Black Dog when he was a young man. He was cycling home one moonlit night from playing in a darts match at a pub in Norwich. As he neared home he saw a huge black dog sitting by the signpost at a crossroads. It had eyes that 'shone like coals of fire' and it began to follow the cyclist. It passed by him so close that he could 'smell its rankness,' stopping at the edge of a wood and was then hit by a passing automobile. Ramsey was astonished to see the Black Dog was still standing after the impact. As he watched in amazement it then vanished (Westwood 2001: 101–102).

A modern story about the sighting of a Black Dog by a Methodist minister, a very reliable eye witness with good social standing, was related by Peter Jeffrey. The minister was driving through an unnamed Suffolk village one night when suddenly a large black dog ran out into the road in front of his car. Unable to swerve out of the way or stop in time the minister's car struck the animal and he felt its wheels go over the body. The clergyman stopped the car and was puzzled to find no sign of the dog in the road even though he was sure he had killed it. He approached an old man who was standing at an adjacent bus stop and asked him if he had seen the black dog. The man replied that he had seen nothing except the minister's car braking sharply and suddenly stopping. When the minister explained what had happened to him the old man smiled and told the clergyman not to worry 'as it happens here regular' (Jeffrey 1988:86).

One of the last reported sightings of Black Shuck was at Bradwell-on-Sea on the Essex coastline in 2002. A man and his son were out one night on the marshes 'lamping' or hunting foxes with the aid of an electric torch and a shotgun. They were walking along the sea wall when a massive 'wolf-like' black dog with a shaggy coat came out of the bushes and crossed the footpath in front of them. They described it as bigger than a deerhound or wolfhound. Some time later they saw the creature again near their house. It emerged from one hedge, crossed the corner of a field and disappeared into another hedge.

In local folklore the East Anglian fens were a demon-haunted landscape believed to be populated by weird elemental creatures. These were described as having large heads with pointed chins, eyes as big as saucers, scaly bodies and crooked legs. They sound very like the *dokklafr* or dark elves from Scandinavian mythology and they may have influenced the East Anglian beliefs about the Pharisees or faery folk. Elves were the spirits of the earth, woods and wasteland where humans feared to tread. In many cases this belief in the Good Folk related to pre-Christian ideas about nature spirits, who were transformed into devils and demons by the Early Church when it suppressed pagan beliefs.

Two examples can be found in Suffolk that illustrate this gradual transition from paganism to Christianity. At Southwold Mere there is a hill where the remains of a circular earthwork were found in the 19th century. Although it was probably a Bronze Age settlement or Iron Age hill fort, the locals insisted it had been built by the pagan Danes when they came to the area. In 1769 an anonymous writer said he had been told by local people that the earthworks were 'fairy hills' and on moonlit nights the Good Folk had been seen dancing there.

When the Christian missionary St Botolph came to East Anglia he decided to build a church on a small island that was surrounded by the marshes. The natives told him that the place was known as the 'hill of the devils' and was demon-haunted. The saint had to exorcise the island and banish its resident spirits before he could build his new church. This suggests the hill had once been the site of the worship of the pagan gods or nature spirits.

In the annals of historical witchcraft in the British Isles witches and faeries were often interrelated. In fact historian Emma Wilby from the University of Exeter in Devon has actually coined the term 'fairy familiar' to describe this relationship and has pointed out that the nature of faeries was ambivalent (Wilby 2005:112). They could be either benevolent and kind to humans or antagonistic and harmful. In this respect they reflected Scandinavian faery lore where there were dark elves as well as light elves. In Scottish witch lore there are many examples of witches working with faeries and using 'elf shot' (prehistoric flint arrowheads) to 'blast' or curse their enemies. A similar symbiotic relationship is also found in the English West Country.

Although East Anglian witchcraft is lacking the extensive faery lore found in Scotland and south-west England there are one or two hints from the period of the trials to a relationship between witches and the Good Folk. In 1499 Agnes Clark said that her daughter Mariana had been given a 'hollow wand' by the faeries. They had also taught her how to heal the sick, predict the future and find buried treasure. Possibly the wand was some kind of dowsing rod. In her innocence Clark took the faery wand to a priest and asked him to bless it. The Witch of Eye, Margaret Jourdemain, was said at her trial to have been able to conjure up both 'fiends' and the faery folk.

One common faery type in Norfolk was variously known as the hytersprite, highty sprightly, hikey sprite or spikey. Sprite means an elf, goblin or pixy, while 'hyter' or 'hikey' is of unknown origin. Ray Loveday, who has carried out research into the modern belief in these entities, believes the word comes from the Anglo-Saxon *hedon* and the Dutch *hoeden* meaning to keep, guard, protect or watch over. Linguistically both words could have come to Norfolk with historical immigrants from Germany and Holland.

Hikey sprites were first mentioned in writing in 1872 by Walter Rye in the *Eastern Counties Collectanea* and were referred to simply as faeries. Modern people interviewed by Ray Loveday during his research also described them as faeries or 'little people about at night time', but also variously as gnomes, demons, elves and goblins. One of Loveday's informants described them as 'a kind of misty thing' and likened them to the Lantern Man, Will O' the Wisp or Jack O' Lantern. These folklore characters were seen at night in the form balls of light floating over the misty marshes and were dismissed in scientific terms as phosphorescent 'marsh gas' or methane released from the ground (Loveday 2009:11–12). In some other countries mysteries balls of light have been seen rising from the ground at geological faults before earthquakes.

Although hikeysprites could be benevolent in nature, the general consensus was that they were evil, mischievous and unpleasant. Norfolk mothers seem to have used them as bogeymen to scare children and prevent them wandering off alone or to get them to come home before it got dark. Alternatively the sprites were used to scare them into behaving because children were told that if they were naughty 'the hikey man will come and get you.' One of Loveday's elderly informants remembers when she was a child and in bed her grandmother shouted up the stairs: 'Put that candle out. If not the hikey sprites will get you' (ibid:19).

The hikeysprite seems to have been a shapeshifter with the power to change form into a bird, usually sand martins. Other descriptions say that in their humanoid form they are about two feet tall with sandy colored skin and green eyes. Yet another description says they are small and thin with unusually long skinny arms and legs, bony skeletal fingers and wear a pointed cap. One eyewitness told Ray Loveday that a hikeysprite had appeared to him as a tall man wrapped in a black cloak.

The most famous case of an alleged intrusion of the faery folk into the material world took place in Suffolk in the 12th century. A boy and a girl, evidently brother and sister, were found wandering near a pit at a village called Woolpits. They seemed to be ordinary children except that their skin had a strange greenish hue and nobody could understand the strange language they spoke. They were taken to the house of a local nobleman, Sir Richard de Calne, where they initially refused the food offered to them. Eventually they accepted some beans, began to eat normally and over time the green colour of their skin faded.

The boy unfortunately died, but his sister learnt to speak English and accepted Christian baptism. She became a servant in Sir Richard de Calne's household, although her conduct was described as 'loose and wanton.' When questioned about where she came from the girl was reluctant to say much. She did reveal that they had come from a subterranean realm where everyone who lived there had green skin. There was no sun but she said the country was illuminated by the type of twilight experienced in the human world immediately before sunrise or after sunset. They had gotten lost one day in this strange country of green people and that is how they ended up in what they called the overworld.

The Ipswich Journal published an article on East Anglian faery lore in 1877. It said that in Suffolk people had described the Pharisees, as they were called, as about the size of mice. They were dressed in blue coats, yellow trousers and red pointed caps with tassels on. In the mid-19th century a man walking home from Bury St Edmunds saw a dozen faeries dancing in a ring in a field. He said they were about three feet high, 'doll like', wearing 'sparkly' clothes and appeared to be 'light and shadowy, not like solid bodies.' He ran the rest of the way home to get his neighbors, but when they returned to the field the faery dancers had gone.

Over a hundred years later in 1982 two primary school children from Jaywick in Essex saw two small figures about three feet tall. They were digging a hole in the school playing field. The girls described them as looking like little old men with long white beards and pointed caps—a description suggestive of gnomes or dwarves. Eleven years later an inhabitant of Boxted awoke during the night to see a shining hexagonal crystal on the bedroom floor. Six gnomish figures were walking clockwise around it. Each was about a foot high with a long white beard and was dressed in green and brown clothing. The pet cat was trying to pounce on the creatures but they were moving too fast for it to catch them (Bord 2004: 56–57).

One of the spirits that haunted the fens and marshes mentioned before in relation to the hikeysprites was Jack O' Lantern or Will O' the Wisp, who was also known as the Lantern Man. In 1810 he was seen by several witnesses at a place called Alder Cair Pen Broad in Norfolk. The manifestation was described as looking like a candle flickering in a lantern and burning with a bright blue and green flame. Despite the fact it was a clear, still night it always twisted and turned as if being blown by the wind. Sometimes the lantern was seen to be carried by a diminutive man wearing a medieval-type tunic and a pointed cap and boots. Travelers crossing the marshes late at night where the spirit lantern had often been seen had their own lanterns wrenched from their grasp by an invisible force and smashed to the ground. One horseman who dared to dismiss Old Jack as a fantasy was knocked off his mount into a ditch. Less superstitious people said that Jack O' Lantern was not a spirit at all. They claimed he was a fantasy figure invented by smugglers to keep the curious away from the sites of their nefarious illegal activities. In south-west England Jack of the Lantern was a regarded as a pixy (faery) and a local version of the god of the witches.

In the historical witchcraft trials the prosecutors always claimed that the suspected witches owed allegiance to and worshipped the Devil. In popular East Anglian folklore Old Nick was often associated with prehistoric standing stones indicating a link with pagan gods like Woden who were worshipped in the area in ancient times. At Clediston in Suffolk a six feet tall standing stone, possibly originally a glacial deposit, stood in the garden of a bungalow. It was on land previously owned by Rockstone Manor and was supposed to have been a 'druidic sacrificial site.'

Originally the standing stone was ten feet high and at least eight feet wide. In popular folk tradition it was connected with appearances of the Devil and for that reason it was shunned after dark. The monolith in fact was called Cledd's Stone and took its name from a missionary bishop who first brought Christianity to the area. In 660 CE he is said to have stamped out the pagan worship of Woden at the stone. With the coming of the new religion this Germanic god (equivalent to Odin in Scandinavia) was often identified with the Devil, especially when he was the male leader of the Wild Hunt.

At Westerton, Suffolk the so-called Witch's Stone was also said to be a place where the Devil could be seen. The stone stands in the churchyard of St Peter's, which dates from the early 14th century. A local folk story says the Devil actually lives under the stone or that his dwelling is underground nearby. It is said that if somebody starts off from the stone and runs three or seven times around the church widdershins (anti-clockwise) then Old Nick will rise out of the ground. One of the vicars of the church dismissed the tradition as just another spooky tale dreamt up by the local smugglers who used to hide their contraband in the church crypt near the stone (Jibson 1971:52).

At Home Farm on the Fardley Hall country estate in Suffolk there once stood a large stone with several cracks in it. Local children would place pins in these cracks and then run or dance around the stone. It was then claimed that the Devil would speak from inside the monolith. Again this may be a far memory of the pagan belief that stones were inhabited by nature spirits. In Anglo-Saxon times clergymen condemned survivals of paganism including the worship of stones and trees. The site at Home Farm was associated with a romantic story about buried pirate treasure and was also said to be the meeting place of a local coven of witches.

St Mary's churchyard at Bungay, the site of an appearance of the demonic Black Dog during a thunderstorm has a small stone in it about two feet high. It is popularly known as either the Devil's Stone or the Druid's Stone. It is romantically claimed it was a druidic altar used for human sacrifices before the church was built. Popular folklore says that if a person ran around the stone seven times on 'a certain day of the year' (unfortunately not specified in the lore) the Devil would appear. In 1934 a local historian claimed the Devil's Stone could be a prehistoric marker on a ley or spirit path that interestingly passed through the church.

In East Anglian folk tradition there are many stories of people selling their souls to the Devil. However in country lore and folk tradition Old Nick was not the satanic bogey and cosmic principle of evil promoted by the Church. Instead he was a folksy trickster figure who could be outwitted by someone, often a cunning person, who was intelligent enough. The nobleman Sir Barnabas Brograve (1726–1797) fitted the archetypal image of the 'wicked squire' who came to a violent end and was condemned to suffer for his sins in the afterlife. On every New Year's Eve at his Norfolk country house Wexham Manor the table was set by his servants for seven, even though Sir Barnabas always dined alone. It was said that at the tuning of the year the aristocrat was joined for dinner by six phantom guests. They were the ghosts of his ancestors who had all died violently in battle.

Sir Barnabas also sold his soul to the Devil and when he came to collect it the cowardly nobleman hid in the windmill at Brograve. The building used to lean heavily to the west and it was said this was caused by the Devil when he tried to blow it over and seize Sir Barnabas' soul. It was popularly known as the Devil's Mill for this reason and its original owner had been a miller who was also a necromancer. Possibly he may have been a member of the rural secret society known as the Miller's Word, whose members were taught and practised sorcery.

In the 1870s a Mrs Tash from Magdalen in Norfolk was supposed to have sold her soul to 'Old Harry' or the Devil when she was only a child. When she was seriously ill in bed and was not expected to live two of her neighbors came to visit her. They found the bed was empty and there were strange claw-like marks on the windowsill. A search party was organized to track down and find the missing woman. Mrs Tash was found the next morning in a pit by the side of a dyke. She was stark naked and alive. However she had been struck dumb with shock and was unable to tell her rescuers what had happened to her. Her last recollection was being tucked up in bed in her cottage.

The old woman was taken back to her cottage and placed back in her bed with her neighbors watching over her. She slept most of the day but in the middle of the next night started to writhe about and shout out incoherently. As the terrified neighbors watched a large black bird of an unknown type crashed into the window plane and tried to gain entry to the bedroom. They ran out of the room to call for help from Mrs Tash's son who was downstairs. When they returned the woman was dead and on her chest was the mark of the talon of some kind of large bird. Everybody said that the Devil must have finally claimed his prize.

Sightings of the Devil were comparatively rare or if they were more common were seldom described or mentioned in print. One exception to the rule was the experience of an Essex man. He claimed to have encountered Old Nick in a country lane while walking home from the pub. He said the Old One was at least seven feet tall, covered in long hair with cloven hooves and had huge ears 'like rhubarb leaves'. When the terrified man arrived home and told his incredulous wife about his horrible experience she accused him of drinking too much.

In the Middle Ages a priest called Father Rainaldus was standing in for the incumbent at Runwell's church (Essex) because he was confined to his sick bed. Rumor had it that the man's replacement was a secret dabbler in the Black Art. This was confirmed when during Rainaldus' first sermon in the church the Devil suddenly materialized to claim his soul. The priest leapt down from the pulpit and ran as fast as he could to the door with Old One in hot pursuit. Unfortunately for the Devil he was traveling so fast that he could not stop. He crashed into the church door that the priest had slammed behind him. Evidence of this infernal collision could be seen afterwards as the Devil's claw marks were visible on the door.

In Christian mythology the Devil was sometimes depicted as a dragon or winged serpent. In Revelations for instance there is a reference to 'the dragon, that old serpent, which is the Devil, and Satan...' (20:2). In 1449 at Little Carnard, where the River Stow provide a natural boundary between Essex and Suffolk, two dragons were seen engaged in mortal combat. People gathered to watch the strange spectacle of the two beasts, one black and one red in color, fighting on the banks of the river. For over an hour they struggled using their teeth and claws to inflict wounds on each other and completely ignoring the watching human audience. To the disappointment of the watchers they finally gave up and in an anti-climax wandered off.

A dragon legend from Wormingfield (Essex) is reminiscent of modern stories about exotic pet owners releasing them into the wild. The story begins in the Holy Land when allegedly King Richard the Lionheart was given the unusual present of a cockatrice. When the king eventually returned to England the dragon-like creature was kept in the royal menagerie at the Tower of London along with the lions, leopards and bears. Unfortunately it escaped and ended up in Wormingfield (*Worm* or *wurm* means flying serpent or dragon in Old English). Because the creature was attacking livestock and decimating the local population of virgins the villagers hired a brave knight called Sir George de la Hye, the son of a French count, to hunt it down and kill it.

In the 12th century a particularly hungry and ferocious dragon was ravaging the countryside around the ancient Saxon town of St Osyth, later famous for its witches. It was described by one witness who survived to tell the tale as of 'marvelous bigness'. In fact it was so large it could demolish a house with one swipe of its barbed and scaly tail. At Ludlam a winged serpent used to emerge from its underground lair after dark to terrorize it inhabitants. As soon as the sun rose the monster slunk back into its hiding place. This led to the belief it was of demonic origin. When the beast was out rampaging one night the villagers rolled a large stone across the entrance to the cave where it lived. When the dragon returned and could not get in it left the area and was never seen again.

In 1668 a dragon suddenly appeared in the Essex village of East Hamdon. According to one account a man out riding was attacked by the creature. He managed to spur on his terrified horse and escape its clutches. Shortly afterwards two men came across the dragon sleeping in the warm sunshine. They described it as having large and piercing eyes, two rows of sharp pointed teeth and two small stubby wings on its back that seemed incapable of the power of flight. One man went off to get help while the other stayed behind to watch the dragon. Unfortunately it woke from its slumber, escaped into a nearby wood and was never see again.

A carved representation of a dragon can be seen in the 14th century church at Henham in Essex. In a pamphlet called *The Flying Serpent of Henham* by Phillip Lillycrap published in 1669 it says a churchwarden, an overseer of the workhouse for the poor and four local householders (i.e., respectable members of the community) all testified to seeing the dragon. It was reported that the creature was living in a wood near the village. It was described as being about nine feet long and having the usual piercing eyes, rows of sharp teeth and purely decorative wings. Although the locals attempted to hunt down the dragon of Henham, it always managed to elude them somehow. It is possible that some of the folklore about dragons is associated with leys or spirit paths. These are sometimes called 'dragon paths' and the earth energy that is believed to flow along them is called 'dragon energy' or the 'breath of the serpent.'

Bibliography

Ady, Thomas. *A Candle in the Dark*. 1656.

Almond, P. C. *The Witches of Warboys*. Taurus, 2008.

Anon. *The Most Strange and Admirable Discoverie of Three Witches of Warboys*. 1593.

Anon. *A True and Faithfull Narrative of Oliver Cromwell's Compact with The Devil*. 1660.

Anon. *The Trial of Witches at Bury St Edmunds*. William Shrewsbury, 1682.

Anon. 'Witches Over the Crouch', *The Times*, 27th January 1959.

Ashton John. *The Devil in Britain and America*. Ward and Dunning 1896.

Athestan, James. 'Witchcraft in Kings Lynn.' *Fate*, April 1965.

Barrett, Francis. *The Magus*. Lackington, Allen & Co., 1801.

Barrett, Pam and Brian Bell. *Insight Guide to England*. Insight Guides, 2007.

Barrett, W.H. and Enid Porter. *More Tales from the Fens*. Routledge & Kegan Paul, 1964.

Bord, Janet. *The Traveller's Guide to Fairy Sites*. Gothic Image 2004.

Briggs, Robin. *Witches & Neighbours*. Fontana Press, 1997.

Chambers, Robert. *The Chambers Book of Days*. W & R Chambers, 1879.

Cobell, Craig. *Witchfinder-General: The Biography of Matthew Hopkins*. Sutton Publishing, 2006.

Coleman, Stanley. *Traditional Lore of East Anglia*. Folklore Academy, 1961.

Collins, Andrew. 'Essex Witchcraft Investigated', *The Cauldron* No. 99, February 2001.

————. 'The Devil in Essex', *The Cauldron* No 108, 2003.

Devereux, Paul. *Haunted Land*. Judy Piatkus Publishers, 2001.

————. *Fairy Paths & Spirit Roads*. Vega, 2003.

Evans, George Ewart. *The Pattern Under the Plough*. Faber & Faber 1966.

————. 'The Horse and Magic', *Pentagram*, 1966.

————. *The Leaping Hare*. Faber & Faber, 1972.

————. *Horse Power and Magic*. Faber & Faber 1979.

Ewen, C. L'Estrange. *Witch Hunting and Witch Trials*. Kegan Paul, Trench and Trubner, 1929.

————. *Witchcraft and Demonianism*. Heath Cranton, 1933.

Davenport, John. *The Witches of Huntingdon*. 1646.

Davies, Dr Owen. *Witchcraft, Magic and Culture 1736–1951*. Manchester University Press, 1999.

————. *Cunning Folk: Popular Magic in English History*. Hambledon-London, 2003.

Deacon, Richard. *Matthew Hopkins: Witchfinder General*. Muller, 1976.

Fernee, Ben. *The Society of the Horseman's Word*. Society of Esoteric Endeavour, 2009.

Forby, Robert. *East Anglian Superstitions*. 1830.

Forman, Joan. *Haunted East Anglia*. Fontana-Collins, 1975.

Gardiner, Tom. *Broomsticks Over Essex*. Ian Henry Publications, 1981.

Gaskill, Malcolm. *Witchfinders: A Seventeenth-Century English Tragedy*. Murray, 2005.

Gifford, George. *A Dialogue Concerning Witches and Witchcraft*. 1593.

Gurdon, Eveline C. *Old Suffolk Lore and Cure Charms*. Pawsey & Hayes, 1893.

————. *County Folk-lore: Suffolk*, 1893.

Gueber, H. A. *Myths of the Norsemen*. 1908.

Glyde, John. *The Folk-lore and Witchcraft of Suffolk*. Jarrold, 1866.

————. *A Norfolk Garland*. Jarrold, 1872.

————. *The Suffolk Garland*. 1866.

Haining, Peter. *The Witchcraft Papers*. Robert Hale, 1974.

Haining, Peter and A. V. Sellwood. *Devil Worship in Britain*. Corgi Books, 1964.

Harris, Antony. *Witch Hunt: The Great Essex Scare of 1582*. Ian Henry Publications, 2001.

Heard, Victor. *Hereward the Wake*. Alan Sutton Publishing 1995.

Hippisley, Cox, R. *The Green Roads of England*. Methuen, 1914.

Hopkins, Matthew. *The Discoverie of Witches*, 1647.

Hole, Christine. *Witchcraft in England*. B. T. Batsford & Co 1977.

Howell, Thomas. *A Complete Collection of State Trials*. Longmans, 1816.

Jackson, Louise. 'Witches, Wives and Mothers', *Women's History Review* 4 (1) Routledge 1995.

Jefrey, Peter. *East Anglian Ghosts, Legends and Lore*. The Old Orchard Press, 1988.

Jennings, Hermoine. 'A Cambridgeshire Witch', *Folk-lore* 16 1905.

Kent, Sylvia. *Folklore of Essex*. Tempus, 2005.

Knightly, Charles. *Folk Heroes of Britain*. Thames & Hudson, 1982.

Lefurbe, Charles. *Witness to Witchcraft*. Ace Star Books, 1970.

Levack, Brian P. *The Witch-Hunt in Early Modern Europe*. Longman Group, 1995.

Liddell, E.W. *The Pickingill Papers*. Capall Bann, 1994.

Loveday, E. Roy. *Hikey-Sprites: Twilight of a Norfolk Tradition*. E. Roy Loveday, 2009.

Laver, Henry. 'Fifty Years Ago in Essex', *The Essex Naturalist* 111. January–June 1889.

Macfarlane, Alan. *Witchcraft in Tudor and Stuart England*. Routledge & Kegan Paul 1970.

Maple, Eric. 'Cunning Murrell', *Folklore* Vol 71, No 1. March 1960.

————. 'The Witches of Canewdon', *Folklore* Vol 7, No 4. December, 1960.

————. *The Dark World of Witches*. Robert Hale, 1962.

————. 'The Witches of Dengie', *Folklore* Vol 76, No. 3. Autumn, 1965.

May, Spike. *Return to East Anglia*. Victor Gollanz 1986.

Morant, Phillip. *History and Antiquities of the County of Essex* 1768.

Morgan, Glyn H. *Essex Witches*. Spurbrook Books, 1973.

————. *Secret Essex*. Ian Henry Publications, 1982.

Morrison, Arthur. 'A Wizard of Yesterday' *Strand Magazine*. 1900.

————. *Cunning Murrell: A Tale of Witchcraft and Smuggling*.1900, Boydell Press, 1977.

Oldridge, Darren. *The Witchcraft Reader—Second Edition*. Routledge, 2008.

Newman, Thomas. *The Arrangement, Judgement and Execution of Three Wytches of Huntingdonshire*. 1593.

Pennick, Nigel. *Daddy-Witch, and Old Mother Redcap*. Cornerstone, 1985.

————. *Skulls, Cats and Witch Bottles*. N.P. Publications, 1986.

————. *Practical Magic in the Northern Tradition*. Thoth, 1989.

————. *Secrets of East Anglian Magic*. Robert Hale, 1995.

————. *Natural Magic*. Lear Books, 2005.

————. *Folk-lore of East Anglia*. Spiritual Arts & Crafts, 2006.

————. *Operative Witchcraft*. Lear Books, 2011.

————. *In Field & Fen*. Lear Books, 2011.

Perkins, William. *A Discourse on the Damned Arte of Witchcraft*. 1608.

Platt, R. *The Ordnance Survey Guide to Smugglers in Britain*. Ordnance Survey, 1991.

Pollington, S. *Leechcraft: Early English Charms, Plantlore and Healing.* Anglo-Saxon Books, 2000.

Porter, Enid. *Cambridgeshire Customs and Folklore.* RKP, 1969.

——————. *The Folklore of East Anglia.* B. T. Batsford Co 1994.

Pugh, B. W., Spiring, P. and S. Bhayi. *Arthur Conan Doyle, Sherlock Holmes and Devon.* MX Publishing, 2010.

Randall, Arthur. *Sixty Years a Fenman.* Routledge & Kegan Paul, 1966.

Rex, Peter. *The English Resistance: The Underground War Against The Normans* Tempus, 2004.

Robinson, Bruce. *Peddars Way and Norfolk Coast Path.* Aurum Press, 2007.

Rosen, Barbara. *Witchcraft in England 1558–1618.* University of Massachusetts Press, 1991.

Russell, J. B. *Witchcraft in the Middle Ages.* Cornell University Press.

Sharpe, James. *Instruments of Darkness; Witchcraft in England 1550–1750.* Hamish Hamilton, 1996.

Stearne, John. *A Confirmation and Discoverie of Witchcraft.* 1648.

Stirling-Taylor, G. R. *Oliver Cromwell.* Jonathan Cape, 1978.

Summers, Montague *The Geography of Witchcraft,* 1926.

——————. *The Discovery of Witches: A Study of Matthew Hopkins.* 1928.

——————. *Witchcraft and Black Magic.* Rider & Company, 1946.

——————. Thomas, Keith. *Religion and the Decline of Magic.* Penguin Books, 1991.

Timpson, John. *Timpson's Country Churches.* Weidenfeld & Nicholson, 1998.

Trubshaw, Bob. *Explore Phantom Black Dogs.* Heart of Albion Press, 2005.

Tully, Clive and Richard Denyer. *The Broads.* The Pevensey Press, 2002.

Valiente, Doreen. *ABC of Witchcraft.* Robert Hale 1973.

Westwood, Jennifer. 'Friend or Foe? Norfolk Traditions of Shuck.' H. R. Davidson, ed. *Supernatural Enemies* Carolina Academic Press, 2001.

Waldron, Dr David and Christopher Reeves. *Shuck! The Black Dog of Bungay.* Hidden Publishing, 2010.

Webster, Sybil. *Canewdon: The Bewitching History and Tales.* Privately printed, France, 2005.

Wilby, Emma. *Cunning Folk and Familiar Spirits.* Sussex Academic Press 2005.

Wright, Pip and Jay. *Witches in and around Suffolk.* Payprint Publishing, 2004.

East Anglian Witches and Wizards was printed at Midsummer 2017 by Three Hands Press. The book is strictly limited to 3,533 copies, comprising 2500 sewn and glued softcover copies, one thousand hardcover copies with colour dust jacket, and 35 hand-numbered copies in full black goat with slipcase.

Scribæ Quo Mysterium Famulatur